"**A fascinating read!** A con
ization of her life's true call
physical death is not the en
encounters and synchronist
ability to communicate with those who have passed.

Kay meticulously brings to life her real story of finding meaning and inspiration along her spiritual journey. Her comprehensive approach to the world of mediumship is very insightful and helpful to even those who haven't yet experienced direct spirit contact."

— Felix Lee Lerma, International Medium

"With candor, humor, and warmth, Kay Fahlstrom opens doors to a world of spirit that is familiar, accessible, and compassionate. Who knew a medium could be so down to earth?"

— Katie Malachuk, author of *You're Accepted* and *Earn It*

"Accessible and beautifully written. Kay is able to put into words experiences on a topic that more people need to know about and try to understand."

— Padma Catell, Ph.D., Licensed Psychologist, Professor Emerita (CIIS), and author of *Drugs and Clients: What Every Therapist Needs to Know* (2nd Ed. Solarium Press) & *Through the Gateway of the Heart* (Eds. Ralph Metzner and Padma Catell, 2nd Ed. 2013)

"*Reborn A Medium* is a great read and very gripping! I was able to relate to it in so many ways. It's a captivating and miraculous account of an 'everyday' person—not a monk living on a hilltop. Kay's comfort flows through her words; reducing our normal human fear of death. It's engrossing and thought provoking—keeping a good balance between the ephemeral and the known. The pace is spot on and the emotion is strong!"

— Stephanie Vlahov, M.S. and author of *The Active Creative Child* (Hohm Press) and *Cleo the Cat and Friends - Perspectives on Politically Correct Parenting* (e book)

"A well-written and engaging story of Kay Fahlstrom's journey to experiencing and understanding the psychic phenomena called mediumship. Kay relates with revealing, easy-to-read, personal occurrences of her psychic mediumship abilities, as well as, demystifies many questions surrounding this paranormal talent. I applaud Kay's genuineness as she takes the reader on a life path which has been filled with synchronicity, intuition, clairvoyance, and compassion."

— Barbara Sinor, Ph.D., author of *The Pact: Messages from the Other Side*

"An amazing journey of discovery. Fahlstrom shares the joys and challenges of discovering and nurturing her newfound talent for communicating with those who have passed on. As she does, it provides a road map for anyone on a similar journey—whether or not they've had to die for it! The book is down-to-earth, practical, and fun to read for both beginner and advanced souls alike!"

— Sue Wilhite, Events Manager, East West Bookshop and author of *21 Templates that Run Your World* and *Setting Up Your Psychic Practice*

"*Reborn a Medium* is both captivating and informative in its use of Kay Fahlstrom's personal journey as a springboard for our collective consideration. Beautifully balanced between anecdotal and didactic, she successfully shepherds the reader through the mysteries of a near-death experience, spiritual awakening and communication with people on the other side. This is a wonderful read for anyone interested in deepening their awareness of both life beyond our five senses and that our consciousness goes on after crossing over."

— Cristin Brew, Licensed Marriage and Family Therapist specializing in Grief Counseling

"I've had multiple readings with Kay Fahlstrom. Every time I leave a reading, I feel closer to my loved ones in spirit! Now that I've read *Reborn a Medium*, I feel a little closer to both Kay and her special gifts. I highly recommend her readings and this book!"

— Anne Perry, Healthcare Executive

REBORN A MEDIUM

REBORN A MEDIUM

A True Story of Dying, Returning, and Serving Spirit and You

KAY FAHLSTROM

Reborn A Medium: A True Story of Dying, Returning, and Serving Spirit and You

Published in the United States by Kay Fahlstrom
Distributed in the United States and Worldwide by CreateSpace.com (a division of Amazon.com)

Project Editor: Linda Jay
Cover Design: Ianziti Design
Interior Design & Layout: Val Sherer

ISBN 13: 978-0-9903787-0-9 (trade paperback)

Library of Congress Control Number: 2014908355

First Edition

To Mary, who encouraged this book into being.

To my mother Dorothy, who encouraged me to finish this book via several messages from the other side. Also, my heartfelt thanks to her for somehow managing to be like two parents rolled into one for me.

CONTENTS

Foreword

Kay Fahlstrom is a sincere messenger for Spirit people who want to come through for their loved ones here. You won't want to miss a page of Kay's journey from nearly dying and returning to her lifeless body, her unfolding path that emerged—including premonitions, psychic ability… then later mediumship—and discovering then embracing the unyielding pull that nudged her off her chosen marketing career in order to be of service as a full-time psychic medium.

Kay and I have gotten to know each other over the last five years as she's taken many of my intermediate and advanced mediumship courses and workshops. In doing so, I can personally relate to her journey as a medium as well as what it's like to survive a near-death experience as I also have.

Two of my passions are serving Spirit and clients directly all around the world as a medium and clairvoyant in front of large audiences, as well as teaching budding advanced psychic mediums all around the world. After the initial Mediumship Workshop Kay attended in late 2009, I next offered courses to assist mediums at different levels of development. So, I next saw Kay in my Intensive Mediumship Workshop held later the next year. I sifted through 100s of applicants to determine the people I felt I should teach in this more advanced course. I got to know Kay better as she later also attended my Advanced

Mediumship Course (again where I chose attendees from a deluge of applications). This rigorous course included a four-week live online course I taught followed by an intensive weekend together where the mediums learned and practiced much, then were tested in two one-on-one live readings with Los Angeles residents. From these live readings, I received direct feedback, along with my observations of the medium attendees, to select the first group of Certified Spiritual Advisors in the Lisa Williams International School of Spiritual Development (LWISSD). Kay nearly screamed my ear off in her excitement of having been chosen by me as a Certified Spiritual Advisor during my phone call letting her know.

There are two memorable moments that come back to me as I write Kay's book Foreword. One was in my Platform Mediumship Course where the attendees, including Kay, had to give messages in front of live audiences. There was a humorous moment early in the first training day where I wanted to bring up an attendee to show something to the rest of the class. Kay knew nothing of this, so the look on her face when I told the rest of the class that "Kay is now going to demonstrate … " was priceless! Kay was wide eyed with shock, and I drew out the moment a bit with my long pause while she wondered what in the world she was going to have to demonstrate. Then, I finished my sentence finally with "Kay is now going to demonstrate … a direct message, or direct hit." A direct message is one given by a medium who knows which audience member their spirit messages are for—so they can start right off with the messages (versus an indirect message where the medium takes some time using the messages to determine what audience member they need to speak with). Kay looked even more shocked at my pronouncement, and then took a deep breath and started to give a messages to a woman she identified in the front row with, "Sandy, would you like a message?" After Sandy said yes, Kay was off and running giving messages from Sandy's loved ones in Spirit. Kay delivers her messages, with both healing and evidential (provable) information, in a very caring and compassionate way. This course culminated with a live audience from the Los Angeles area so eight medium attendees could give messages to that live audience from the stage with microphone in hand. Kay was one of those eight mediums, and I took detailed notes on what pieces of information came through that audience members could verify, so I could give the mediums feedback. This was one of those memorable moments from the several courses Kay's taken with me as I encouraged all the mediums to take their skills to the next level—which is a never-ending kind of *staircase up* when you are a medium as we are all developing mediums continuing to hone our skills with each message we give.

Another moment that comes to mind as I write this was from the Advanced Mediumship Course noted above. Kay was receiving a message from another attendee. It was Kay's uncle in Spirit coming through to her about getting this book finished and out to the public. Kay flopped back in her chair with surprise at this validating message from the Other Side, as she was just talking at lunch with a friend about how she wanted to finish this very book. I recall quickly tuning in to see if I received any impressions about her book, and said out loud to the whole class, "The book is going to be published, by the way." Kay looked gob smacked. So, it's fitting I'm able to write this Foreword as I've been aware this book was being written for some time (with encouragement from the Other Side)!

This book will help anyone who: is having intuitive experiences and trying to make sense of them; is simply curious about a person who lived through a harrowing near-death experience; or may even feel pulled to a different kind of work (or volunteer work) than one is doing now. In Kay's case, she feels clearly that she was given a new mission during her near-death experience, yet ironically—like many other near-death experiences noted by published authors—one is not always allowed to directly recall the near-death experience or their personal mission (but rather come upon glimpses of it over time as one's life unfolds). Through intuitions, and a growing relationship with her own spirit guides, Kay came to see that becoming a medium seemed to be an inevitable outcome after her near-death experience. So Kay, after studying and being in development circles for years, embraced this calling fully after doing volunteer readings for clients on nights and weekends around her full-time work in another field, so she could then later make the seamless transition to "being of service" as a full-time medium for Spirit and you.

You may have noticed that some mediums *are born* and grow up having experiences with Spirits from a young age. Other people like Kay, become mediums as a result of somehow surviving their near-death experience. It's well documented that near-death experiences are life-changing, as I personally know from having one myself. Read this behind the scenes account of dying and coming back. Kay's fateful near-death night clearly created a new direction (or mission, if you will) in her life … as near-death experiences often do. She likens having this second chance at life, and her new unchartered path that followed, as being *Reborn a Medium*. You may relate to having intuitions, like Kay does, or feel pulled by a different kind of work (paid or volunteer) in this lifetime. This book with help you with either as you may glean from its pages how to use your intuitions to assist you in getting closer to a life that may more closely line up with your true nature—your soul. Join Kay on her journey from receiving a *new life* (and mission) to coming full circle to be of service as a medium for Spirit and people like you.

LISA WILLIAMS

PART I

TO DEATH AND BACK

Chapter 1

My Near-death Experience

Fall was quickly turning to a bitingly cold winter in Kalamazoo, Michigan where I'd lived for less than a year after landing my first job after college. I was enjoying living in my very own apartment after happily growing up in a bustling Wisconsin household full of siblings and pets. I was also adjusting to my first real job, living on my own, and dealing with all that goes with that transition. My days were busy and my mind filled with so many things, so when the winter chill came on in full force, I just turned up the heater and kept bustling forward.

I had planned to visit a friend back in Madison, Wisconsin on my days off one week. I had completed my evening shift at the local television news station, where I distributed the final scripts for each newscaster and worked behind-the-scenes as floor director (cueing the talent when the camera was about to go on-the-air live or go to a commercial) or running the teleprompter.

I planned to visit my friend after my night shift, knowing that my drive to Madison would be much faster if I could simply zip through the Chicago freeways in the middle of the night, rather than in the daytime. Having done this before, I knew it would shave *hours* off the trip, compared to how long it would take through heavy daytime freeway traffic. I was excited to go visit my friend, but all week, I had been suffering from terrible headaches. As the days went by, my headaches were getting more intense and I also started to have flu-like symptoms—worsening headaches, feeling exhausted and just simply out of it. I thought I had a flu bug, so I postponed the trip, choosing instead to just stay home to try and get better.

Little did I know what a big decision that turned out to be!

Disappointed about not being able to visit with my friend, I headed home after work at midnight to take care of myself and get some sleep. By the time I got home, my headache had turned into an excruciating pain that felt like a vise squeezing my entire head. This was like no other flu bug I had ever had, and I was trying to think of what might alleviate my symptoms and pain.

I was in my early twenties back in the mid 1980s so my main sources of information were family, friends, and news and magazine articles (as there was no Internet to jump on and look up your symptoms and what to do about them … if you can remember that far back). I vaguely remembered reading something in a magazine earlier about possibly being able to decrease pain by using ice on key points in the body to decrease the dilation of blood vessels and blood flow (in hopes that it would decrease this ever-worsening headache). This was all from memory at this point, as I was in agony—so

I'm certainly not advocating this as a remedy. So, there I was, trying to put ice cubes on the veins on my inner wrists (as that's what I recalled from the article I read months before). It didn't help. I can recall glancing in the mirror before heading to bed to try and sleep. My face looked incredibly flushed.

I felt sluggish … almost drugged and chalked it up to being tired after working all week, and this flu. It was about 2:00 a.m. Without ever thinking of getting medical help—as I just had the flu—I just crawled into bed to try and sleep … thinking that would help me feel better by morning. My little grey teenage cat, Scooch, usually slept with me, but for some reason that night only … she was nowhere to be seen. Before zonking out into a deep sleep, I noticed how weird I felt—completely disoriented and totally exhausted. I couldn't even lift my arms anymore to shift position in bed. I went out—cold.

As it turned out, I didn't know I had an intruder in my apartment that evening. A colorless, odorless gas had been wafting through my place all week and had started to build up in my body, increasing my discomfort and adding to my ever-worsening headaches, disorientation and nausea. Little did I know, I was getting a slight break from the deadly gas when I went to my eight-hour shifts at the television station. But now, by cancelling my visit out of town, I unwittingly wrote myself a prescription for death that night.

I'd come to find out later that the landlord must have installed a new heater at some point during the summer or early fall. I had only just begun using the heater since moving in during the summer, as the weather had only just turned cold enough to flip it on. I would also come to find out that the heater had been vented improperly, so that carbon monoxide gas was flowing into my apartment. What's more, I was actually cranking up the heater, as it was getting colder outside and I thought the heat would help me get over what I thought was the flu.

I knew nothing of the symptoms of gas poisoning, so I had no idea what was happening. Carbon monoxide has no smell, so I didn't know I was coming ever closer to death by staying in the apartment. I did not know I should have left immediately. The more carbon monoxide gas I breathed into my lungs, the less oxygen my entire body had with which to function.

Sleep had long taken over and my body was a limp, exhausted mass—probably trying to use what little oxygen I had left to maintain my heart and brain function. At some point in the middle of the night, my consciousness (or soul), needed to leave my body as the carbon monoxide steamrolled through it. I no longer had enough oxygen to function. I was now on the other side of the veil, where people pass away to (or cross over) when their body dies.

What I know is that while out of my physical body, I interacted with other beings that were like loving mentors who had my best interests at heart. I knew I'd have to return to my body, and I felt like I was being given a new agenda—if you will—to work on in my "new life."

You may relate to knowing that *you know* something to be true even though you realize that it's hard to share or explain to another person so that they really *get* what you are saying. My near-death experience ("NDE") is like that. I know what I experienced, as it feels etched like a kind of compass, or blueprint, inside me. I also know that my life changed as a result of leaving my body that night and interacting with benevolent beings on the other side telling me I had to go back and giving me that new blueprint, due to my accidental carbon monoxide poisoning.

Since this life-changing NDE, I've been on several radio programs to share my story and also sometimes give readings to listeners who call in, connecting them with their loved ones who have passed away. I was on one such interview about my near-death experience, and as I lamented about not remembering the much-written-about kind of NDE of the white-light tunnel, meeting your other relatives in spirit, and more, the wonderful interviewer really hit the nail on the head when she spontaneously said, "We die and are allowed to come back into our body … and *even with that miracle,* it's never enough for us, is it?!"

Her remarks stopped me in my tracks. She was right. It WAS enough to die, and be able to come back into my body to live again—as I will share next with you. It was so refreshing to hear someone say that. There are many near-death experience books out there that are wonderful in their full experience of the other side. Even though many of us are allowed to live again after our near-death experiences, some of us wish we could share more of what we experienced.

For whatever reason, I was only allowed to remember coming back in to my body in that Michigan apartment bed. I know that I had an experience on the other side, but perhaps it's because of the lack of oxygen in my brain that I could not process the full near-death experience, or maybe I simply was not "supposed to" remember it to share. I also know—as I write this many years later—that I was being allowed back into my body if I would serve. That's right. On the other side I was told that my "new life" would include trying to be of service to others. It would take me several years to get the experience and training to do so. But, I came to know over the years that followed my NDE—that this was the agreement made on the other side. Did I know this at that point of coming back to my body? Not at all. Why?

Many years after my near-death experience, I happened upon Jan Price's *The Other Side of Death* book.[1] She did have a near-death experience where she recalls many wonderful things about being on the other side, yet still notes what she learned from a wise being she interacted with there as he said to her (in Chapter 5):

"Much knowledge will be received, but **you will not be consciously aware of all of it at the moment. It will be assimilated and brought into remembrance bit by bit after you return to the body.** More understanding is needed there, and you will have the opportunity to share. Beloved old friends will continue to work with you, as we have in the past." (The words in bold are my highlighting.)

Similarly, Betty J. Eadie writes in her book *Embraced By The Light*[2] of her near-death experience and specifically trying to decide whether to come back to earth or stay on the other side. She was informed before learning more about her mission (what she was to be doing here on earth)—what would happen with her memory of her mission if she returned to earth as she writes:

"Your mission will be made known to you so that you might make a clearer decision. But after this, you must decide. If you

[1] Fawcett Columbine/Ballantine Books, 1996, New York, New York

[2] Gold Leaf Press, 1992, Placerville, California

return to your life on earth, your mission and much of what you have been shown will be removed from your memory."

Betty J. Eadie then writes she was shown her mission and knew that she had to come back. She goes on to say the wise being she was interacting with on the other side "… reminded me that when I returned to earth I would not remember what I had seen concerning my mission. 'While on the earth you are not to dwell on what your mission is,' he said. 'It will be done according to its time.' "

Betty J. Eadie writes in the next paragraph, "The details of my mission have been removed from my memory. Not even a hint remains, and strangely, I have no desire to dwell on it."

The Kindness of Strangers

The only reason you are reading these words is due to the kindness—and determination—of a stranger. Having only just moved to this little Michigan town a few months earlier for my first job out of college, I didn't have throngs of friends calling or checking in with me just yet. I wasn't even pals with my downstairs neighbor Cheri, but we were friendly—like ships passing in the night—as we went to and from our jobs and errands. My family and friends in Wisconsin were dear to me then (and are now); but their not hearing from me for a few days was no cause for alarm.

So, there I was … upstairs in this little rental house with two apartments—one downstairs and one upstairs, where I lay. I was gone. I was toast. Dead. My organs, heart, brain—the whole shooting match—could no longer function. Had it not been for one person—the only person who could possibly save me in that entire town—I never would have seen the light of day again, or met my one-and-only dear nephew, or enjoyed my mother for her next 23 years on the planet, or had lovely holidays with my six siblings and their families, or countless other things I am so very grateful to have had. You get the idea. I was very lucky to live to enjoy some experiences I cherish in my new, or second, life.

The next thing I knew—as my body lay lifeless in that upstairs bed—I heard something off in the distance, but it sounded muffled and far away. My consciousness was still out of my body at that point—and it fascinates me now to notice that I could still hear that far off sound (even though I wasn't using my old bodies' physical ears). The part of myself that is aware of being "me" … was out of my old body that could no longer function. One way to think of consciousness is, it's the part of you that is aware you are "in there" when you wake up and look out of your eyes in the morning.

As I tuned my hearing in, I started to get that the sound I heard was a voice. What's more, this voice was yelling! Out of my curiosity of what was being said … still totally unclear on who was saying it … I started to hear instructions from that female voice.

"Kay! Get up and open this door! I KNOW YOU ARE IN THERE! Listen to me … GET UP AND OPEN THIS DOOR! You can do it! C'mon, get up and OPEN THIS DOOR OR I WILL HAVE IT BROKEN DOWN!"

My neighbor, Cheri, who lived downstairs, was shouting directions at me through the outer door to my apartment (at the top landing of wooden stairs between our little flats). The more I tuned in to her voice—in the far distance—I began to absorb what she was saying. She was giving me simple instructions.

Hearing them made me want to do what she was telling me to do … but I couldn't just yet. She was coaching me on the next step to take, and my initial curiosity on what this sound was in the distance made me want to come closer. I was motivated by what she was saying. Brilliant. Cheri had become my lifeline.

I was still completely out of my physical body at that point.

Hearing Cheri screaming, and relentlessly pounding on the door, I tried to do what she was saying. But still, I couldn't yet. I had to bridge the distance from where I was to even begin to follow her orders. I knew I was far away from where I wanted to be. I tried to come back toward the sound … toward my body. Compared to where my consciousness had just been, I now started to enter a point where the energy became thicker and heavier, yet I knew I had to get through that in order to come fully back into my body.

Thanks to Cheri's clear instructions, I was very motivated to bridge this distance. It was not easy. I had to struggle and strain to make it back — to push into the density of our earth world and my body, having just been in the much higher vibration of (simply) consciousness. It felt like the substance I had to get through to get back onto the earth plane was like the thickness of melting tar. My consciousness had to kind of swim through the consistency of tar! This did not just last for a second or two. It was like I had to move slowly through many yards of this melted tar-like substance, or energy, to get back in. It took great effort and concentration to keep pushing forward toward my old body. I concentrated intensely and pushed with all my might! Compared to the lighter, faster, and finer energy of the other side (or spirit world), our energy here on earth is much heavier, thicker, and slower moving (perhaps because actual molecules are moving more slowly to make the form of our bodies, cars, furniture, and the like).

To better understand this difference in the rate of vibration between our world and the other side, I often use the simile of hummingbird wings moving so fast you can scarcely see them to the high, fast fine energy like the other side. Those on the other side (or afterlife, heaven, whatever you like to call it) can be at a much lighter and higher vibration because they don't need the form of bodies, cars, or furniture anymore. Another way to think of this is how an old box fan's blades can spin so quickly you cannot even see them, but you know they are there. The other side is going so fast that we may not be able to see or perceive it but it's also really there. I had to push back into the thick, heavy density of our world in order to get back in to my old body still full of carbon monoxide gas. I kept pushing through that heavy, tar-like energy, as I was so motivated to come back.

Suddenly, I opened my eyes! All my struggle and effort between our worlds was bridged. I was back! I was back in one piece—consciousness and body back together, like we are used to experiencing each day.

Since I was back in my body that was polluted with carbon monoxide, when I followed Cheri's orders and sat up to swing my legs to the side of the bed, it took effort. I was in a bizarre state of being—the only way I can describe it from my limited experiences with altered states of consciousness is I felt like I was way passed intoxicated (not that I had much experience with that). I tried to stand and walk confidently toward the front door to follow Cheri's helpful instructions to open the door. But my legs were like rubber and my upper body like a well-boiled noodle and I fell against the bedroom wall. I'm sure Cheri heard the loud THUD, as at that point I was only about nine feet away from her at the front door.

Cheri, bless her heart, was still shouting to me. "C'mon, Kay! I know you can get over here. Listen to me and get over here and unlock this door!" I steadied myself with my hands and arms and kind of crawled along the wall to the bedroom doorway to the living room entrance. I held both sides of the door frame and leaned into the wall that went along the right side of the living room to the apartment front door.

As I did this, my eyes focused for a second on the living room floor and I saw my little grey cat, named Scooch. She was like a limp dish towel, lying on the living room carpeting. I saw that she had gotten sick on the carpet in many places. Through my mental haze, still impaired by the carbon monoxide poisoning, my brain registered the thought *Oh my God, it's not just me that's ill. Something bad is IN HERE affecting both of us!*

After I opened the front door lock, Cheri helped me open the door and kindly led me down the wooden stairs, acting as my human crutch, so I could get outside then into the backseat of her car. After she poured my five foot, nine inch frame in, I said to her, "My cat … my cat is still up there. Can you please go get her?" Now, my cat was not fond of riding in the car, but I could see something was horribly wrong in that apartment and Scooch was also quite ill so I wanted to get her outside of there … still not even clear on what was really happening.

Cheri was an angel. She ran back into the door and pounded up those wooden stairs to go into my unlocked apartment and grabbed my dear cat up in her arms, raced back down, and put my cat in the backseat with me. Scooch's pretty yellow eyes looked weird … unfocused. I'm sure my eyes looked just as weird. I had no idea what was happening, or even where we were going.

I do not remember the ride to wherever we were going … I must have fallen asleep or gone unconscious during the ride. The next thing I remember was looking up at two nurses who were standing by the bed I was lying on. I registered that I was in a hospital environment (but had no recollection of how I got in there). One nurse stood over me with a clipboard near my shoulders. She asked me what phone number she should call to let someone know where I was. I still didn't know what happened, but I mustered enough energy to tell her the phone number, only—like when I tried to stand up in my bedroom—I was surprised at what happened next.

I wanted to reel off the phone number I had my entire life … from when I grew up in Wisconsin (before going off to college at Madison). But as I opened my mouth, only the first digit came out … *as slow as molasses in a January* in winter, as the old saying goes. I could only sound out "four …." Saying the next digit … even though I knew that phone number my entire life … took a minute or two. Finally I said "three …" and then this slow recall went on for several minutes. When I finally got the entire number out, she turned on her heel and briskly walked away. I knew that childhood phone number my whole life, and I could not get the digits out of my memory bank and into my voice and mouth in order to say each number. Just like swimming in that tar-like substance, I had to work hard to first find each digit then figure out how to get it to my mouth, and then say it. It felt like trying to climb a mountain … a lot of effort.

At this time, I became aware that two men were standing near the foot of my bed. If you like, imagine your favorite hospital television show with a younger, handsome doctor saying to the older, gray-haired doctor, "… but she's still way past textbook death according to the amount of carbon monoxide that is still in her body. How can she be conscious? Why is she still alive?" They must have done a quick test of my blood to determine the amount of carbon monoxide still inside me. I have no recollection of what happened before I was asked for that phone number. Had they pricked my arm for blood? I saw the older doctor kind of shrug his shoulders, as if to say, "I don't know." He said they should get me immediately to the hyperbaric chambers at the hospital across town. I'd later learn that hyperbaric chambers are used to treat carbon monoxide poisoning by forcing pure oxygen back into a poisoned body.

Meanwhile, my sweet cat, Scooch, was still out in Cheri's car, and had only fresh air—no hyperbaric chambers—with the car windows cracked open to try to revive her.

I vaguely remember only the first minute or two of that ambulance ride that ferried me from one Kalamazoo hospital to the other. After that moment of awareness, I became asleep or unconscious again. The next thing I knew, I was lying on a stretcher and the attendants were getting me ready for the hyperbaric chamber treatment and asking me questions. Their questions tested how impaired my brain (and entire body) was at that moment.

I recall being asked to count backwards from the number 100 by eights. What? I have a little trouble with that even when I am fully oxygenated! When I thought I was doing pretty well and got back into the 80s (from the starting point of 100), they stopped me. Apparently, I wasn't doing so well. This was disappointing, because I thought I was nailing it! I was still pretty much toast mentally, at this point.

Next, the attendants in the hyperbaric ward started to ask me POLITICAL QUESTIONS! What? That was just not fair. That was a low blow. How could they assume that anyone with carbon monoxide poisoning could possibly answer political questions?! If my brothers or sisters were lying there, I bet they could have answered these kinds of questions (if fully oxygenated), but me … uh-uh. Those medical professionals were testing my cognitive functioning by asking historical political questions. I was—at that moment—double toast—as I'd be if I were in a "Double Jeopardy!" game show round!

One of the questions they asked was, "How did Gerald Ford become President of the United States?" And, in my carbon monoxide-induced mental haze, I could not answer. I was only around ten years old when that happened.

I was then transferred from my stretcher to a long cookie sheet-like tray that was just about as wide as my 22-year-old body and barely long enough for me. They slid me, like a pan of cookies, into a hyperbaric chamber that was like a cylindrical plastic tube that just barely contained my body. My elbows were uncomfortably squished into the chamber. I could not move. Are you claustrophobic? I am. So I was miserable. It kept running through my head that I would have to endure this weird claustrophobic space for HOURS! I had to remember that this treatment was needed, and try to relax. Ha! I learned later that the point of this chamber was to force pure oxygen into me in order to allow the carbon monoxide, which was still at deathly levels, to exit. So, my discomfort and claustrophobia had to take a back seat.

I had to lie in there and be treated for four hours. Even though my body and mind were out of it, I was still aware of being trapped. I could shout through the Plexiglas-like material, so when the nurses or attendants in that room would walk around to check on me, I made the mistake of asking them how long I needed to be in there. After initially freaking out about the time I had to stay in there … I quickly passed out again. When your body is full of a poison, it shuts you down to try and repair itself … so I could not seem to stay awake in there.

There would be several more treatments of three to four hours like this to come over the coming days, even after I went home after this first treatment. So, imagine: being sent home with a body and a brain that are still not working because of the remaining amount of carbon monoxide inside them. I could not think clearly. I could not balance my checkbook, or, for example, put things in any kind of sequential order (as I had to do for my job to organize the graphics that would go into the newscast). All I wanted to do was sleep … so my body could repair itself to the best of its abilities. I was exhausted all the time and couldn't do anything more than what I absolutely HAD to do that day. Then, I slept more as my body tried to heal itself.

Even in my state, I knew enough to be concerned and I had questions about all of it. When would I ever be done with these treatments? Would I be able to recover to hold a job like I had before? Might I never recover fully and need to move to an assembly-line kind of job for my livelihood? If so, was the four years of incredibly hard work at college in Madison all just a waste of time and energy (not to mention, money)?! This last thought kind of sent me over the edge. These thoughts I had to entertain for more than a week as I received more hyperbaric chamber treatments to try to get the remaining carbon monoxide out of my body to see what kind of recovery I would make for the long term.

Each session of hyperbaric chamber treatment included my breathing pure (100 percent) oxygen in the pressurized chamber; its compression allowed the oxygen to enter my smaller blood vessels and tissue. This additional oxygen was carried throughout my body by my blood to aid in the recovery process. The end goal was, of course, to get my brain (and heart?) functioning at its best again.

As I was going through these separate, three to four hour, claustrophobic hyperbaric chamber treatments, I wondered when they would ever end. I started to realize, as my brain function improved with more oxygen in it after each treatment … they would let me go without more treatments when I could answer the attendants' questions in that treatment ward. So one day while stuck in that plastic tube, being pumped full of pure oxygen … it must have been the fourth treatment or so … I had an epiphany! Then, I knocked on the plastic wall of the chamber to get the attendant's attention, as if to say "Please come over here!" When he did, I shouted through the plastic walls of that long cylinder, "Gerald Ford became president because Richard Nixon resigned!" The attendant smiled, and then turned on his heels to shout to his co-workers across the ward, "She's getting *smarter* in there!"

I came to this answer as with more oxygen in my brain I

could somehow remember, all of a sudden, a pathway of memory back to that time when I was just 10 years old. Because there was no Internet at the time where I could simply look up this historical information ... I actually had to recall this event back up on my own. Because I was so incredibly exhausted between treatments, I didn't even think to "cheat" and ask my older siblings what the answer was. As I lay in the hyperbaric chamber that day, I suddenly remembered back to that younger age where I'd been playing with my friend that lived two blocks away from my childhood home, and suddenly my buddy's mom popped her head out of the house and said we should come in to the house right away. We did and she sat us down in front of the television. She said this was historic and important that we see it. We watched the speech Richard Nixon gave as he resigned the presidency. This memory pathway could be followed again with the better ratio of oxygen to carbon monoxide now in my body during that particular treatment.

Fortunately—after many treatments—my brain function improved to where it had been before. I could even count backward from 100 by eights now! Indeed, I was happy I could do my job at the television station without errors after the final treatment, as I'd previously been making simple mistakes, understandably, between that first and final treatment. I stopped trying to prepare myself for a completely different kind of life. Even though I could think much more clearly now, I still felt oddly different emotionally after my near-death experience.

Why? I wondered. Why did a person like Cheri help me? How did she even know I needed help? Without this determined stranger, I never would have had so many life experiences between the age of 22—the night I almost slipped to the other side forever—and now. I will be forever grateful for the kindness of my neighbor Cheri, who saved my life.

Cheri was a nurse and worked at one of the local hospitals. After this whole ordeal, and in the early days of my becoming mobile and functional again after my treatments, I seem to recall learning that Cheri—during that same fateful week, also suffered from headaches. After she had her blood tested and learned that she had a higher-than-normal level of carbon monoxide in her blood, which was likely adding to her headaches, she then returned to her apartment, which was below mine. She must not have known if the deadly gas was coming from her car, or her living space, or where.

Again, since we're not in touch now (as I moved out of that apartment right after my near-death experience, or "NDE"), the only way I can make sense of this whole chain of events and what may have motivated Cheri to help me is she did know my days off from the television station were Tuesday and Wednesday, since I helped with the weekend evening newscasts. And, living in this small house, I'm sure she could hear the footsteps of both Scooch and my own large, tall frame walking around above her. Perhaps when she didn't hear me or the cat walking around, or hear me get up to do my usual errands as I did on my days off . . . she put two and two together.

Perhaps another reason that has been suggested to me by radio interviewers (well after I had this experience) is more accurate. Perhaps something else moved Cheri into action to try and save my life. Maybe she felt a kind of sudden intuition, or nudge that something was amiss and she should try to intervene in a positive way. Either way, Cheri knew that my car was parked at the house, and I was silent. I'm quite sure she could piece all that together. But what made her actually run up the stairs to try and call in to me?

Maybe it was because she was a nurse and knew what might full well be happening, having known about her carbon monoxide levels that same week. Maybe it was just because she was kind and determined to help, knowing that if I was also suffering from carbon monoxide poisoning, that there would only be a certain window of time where she could do anything to save my life. Maybe it was both. I can't tell you how grateful I am. I'm not the only one—as I recall how my family sent a huge bouquet of roses to Cheri—a total stranger to them—when they learned how she saved my life.

The Feather Landing Softly

If you have ever seen a feather float to the ground, gracefully … that is what this part of my near-death experience feels like. A lovely gift I was given from … I honestly don't know from where.

I do know now that everyone seems to want to know this part of my story. My beloved grey kitty, Scooch, lived through the carbon monoxide poisoning, too (and went on to a ripe old age, I am very happy to say). When people hear or read my story, some lean forward with urgency in their voice and say, "… but what happened to the cat?!" It's funny to me now. I guess I'm just chopped liver. That's why I include my cat in this story. People seem more relieved sometimes to learn that she lived than that I lived. I think it's kind of funny now when people ask, "… but what about your cat … did she live!?" I love animals and I get it. Honestly, it makes no logical sense why either of us made it back to this world and could still function. There seemed to be larger forces at work bringing us both back to life, literally.

Chapter 2

The Journey Begins

Relatively new friends who lived in Kalamazoo expressed concern as they could see the evidence of what I'd been through. Little veins and capillaries on my face had come to the surface (as a result of them kind of screaming out for more oxygen that was needed that night as I breathed in more and more choking carbon monoxide). Even now, I'm still quite ruddy in complexion, and my face can become quite flushed if I accidentally ingest sulfites, which I'm allergic to. My veins and capillaries have had quite a work out in this lifetime … and the history of it still shows. Still, I'm so grateful to have lived. I'd rather have a ruddy complexion for a lifetime and have my brain work than the opposite scenario.

My family back home and out-of-state friends were very concerned and caring when I told them in phone calls about my carbon monoxide poisoning and the aftermath of treatment. I'm not sure any of us really grasped how very close to death I was that night … and that I was already out of my body during the experience. However, I just kept trying to move forward.

I was so thankful that one new friend let my cat and me stay at her place right after the event, as I didn't want to stay in the apartment where the near-death experience (NDE) had occurred. I looked for a new place to live after work hours. Then a helpful, encouraging attorney appeared to try to recover the costs of my medical bills from my landlord. When he heard me report that my landlord had verbally let me out of my lease in a phone call—seeming to understand that I didn't want to spend another night in that apartment—the lawyer thought that part of the case was a slam-dunk for me. Therefore, he was stunned when the judge found in favor of the landlord: that my lease should be upheld and that I was breaking my lease to move. The landlord had changed her tune in court (compared to what she said in the phone call with me) and said I needed to continue with my apartment lease. The lawyer was incredulous at this. But I could not imagine sleeping in that bedroom again. I had to move out for my peace of mind … and I did.

After the NDE, I didn't feel like the same happy-go-lucky young woman that I'd always been. I knew I needed to do something for myself. I was feeling very introspective, as I tried to make sense of what had happened. Before the incident, I would run around, play sports, go jogging, and was excited to meet new people in town. Coming slowly back to life after my NDE, I was simply trying to figure out what might help me most. I was completely introspective—all of a sudden—and just wanted to hole up at home. To take one small step back out into the world, I decided to take a local pottery class. I'd briefly used a potter's wheel in a college art course and had enjoyed it.

Kneading clay and trying to create something beautiful might help me during this quiet phase. I didn't seem to know how to express to others what I had been through—as I've learned since can be difficult for other NDE survivors—so I thought taking this class might help me to integrate nearly dying with being given a second chance at life. It kind of felt weird to be back. My life felt different. At that time, however, I couldn't have told you just how though.

I remember going home to Wisconsin for Christmas to be with my family. I drove the long trip around enormous Lake Michigan, south through Chicago, back up northward through Milwaukee, then on to my mom's house in Green Bay, Wisconsin. It felt really good to see everyone in my large family—three brothers, three sisters, assorted pets, and my mom (my dad passed away when I was nine years old). Apparently I had lost a lot of weight because I had been so ill through the NDE and (uncharacteristically) didn't feel like eating much afterward. It felt a little weird when my brother's friends told me how good I looked because I was thinner (due to the reason why I'd lost weight). I enjoyed being with my family, as I wasn't very established yet with a solid circle of friends in Kalamazoo, having been there only six months.

So, after returning to Kalamazoo for the New Year ahead, I went back to work and looked forward to my pottery class. It was very healing for me to get my hands in the clay, and really learn how to spin and use a potter's wheel to make pots, cups, and vases. I could be quiet and let the whole NDE process through my mind, body and emotions. This pottery class was 'just what the doctor ordered' so to speak … even though I ordered it. I decided I needed to do this … perhaps it was an early intuition, as I was introspective and not ready to run around meeting new people (as I had been before that NDE night). My life had abruptly taken an unexpected detour because of my near-death.

I found a new place to live about a half mile down the hill from my old place. One night I had an unusually vivid dream in my new apartment. As a teenager in Wisconsin, I was not aware of, or familiar with, playing the lottery. So, I'd never seen a lottery ticket in my life. But in my dream, a printer was moving from left to right to print the black on one row, and then it whipped back to the left and moved down one row to print the next line. I could see the lottery ticket taking shape and noted the numbers, which were etched into my mind.

The next day, I leapt out of bed, excited that my mom was flying in that day to visit me. I scurried around, buying groceries and flowers, and got ready to pick her up at the airport. Mom wanted to take a little tour of where I worked at the television station.

As I raced across the small town to pick her up at the local airport, I saw a "Buy LOTTERY Tickets Here" sandwich board outside a convenience store and, for the first time in my life, thought about pulling over to buy a lottery ticket. I zoomed through that green light intersection and past the quickie mart store, thinking to myself, *Should I buy a lottery ticket, since I had that dream last night? Oh, I probably don't have a dollar in my pocket and I don't want to be late for picking up mom at the airport anyway … so I guess I won't.* I liked to be on time. So I greeted mom at the airport and we drove to the TV station.

After mom and I toured most of the station, we sat in the production room with the 6:00 p.m. news director, Jim, whom

I liked, as he was both a good director and fun to be around. Part of my job at the television station was to air the winning lottery numbers between the beginning of the "Jeopardy!" game show but before the first commercial break. This meant quickly calling the Michigan Lottery as soon as possible after the show started at 7:30 p.m. (when the numbers became available), then running to the vidifont machine and quickly typing in the numbers, saving that page, then superimposing the winning numbers over the bottom of "Jeopardy!" before the first commercial started at 7:35 p.m. I had to do a quick little maneuver to get the numbers on and off the screen in time (as you could not have them up over the first commercial).

Just before calling the Michigan Lottery to jot down the numbers, I casually mentioned to Jim and my mom that I saw the lottery numbers in my dream as they printed out onto a ticket. I said out loud the numbers I had seen, and then shuffled into the sound-proof booth where we taped recordings and did live voiceovers at times. It was easy to use the phone in that little glass-walled room. I dialed the lottery recording hotline number. As I did, my face turned white as a ghost. I stumbled back out of the booth to tell Jim and mom that the lottery numbers I'd dreamt of last night were correct!

Upon seeing Jim and mom's incredulous expressions, I slumped into a chair in the production room … shocked. Jim kindly jumped up to assist me with a chuckle, saying, "Don't worry, Kay, I'll do this for you tonight." Mom just seemed to enjoy the hoopla of this whole experience unfolding. Jim put the winning lottery numbers up before the deadline, then looked at me and asked, "Well … did you buy a ticket?" After I explained I didn't because I wanted to be punctual for mom's arrival, he said through warm laughter, "Kay, the next time you dream the lottery numbers, tell ME … and *I'LL buy the ticket* if you don't!"

The next day, mom and I marveled at the events of the night before, and I heard her on the phone telling family back in Wisconsin and Minnesota the story, in a very animated way. I pondered this unusual experience long after she went back home to Wisconsin. I realized everything, beginning with the obvious: I never "asked" for the winning lottery numbers, as I wasn't even *aware* of, or interested in, the lottery. However, it was clear to me that it was part of my job at the television station to post the lottery numbers for Michiganders to feverishly check their purchased lottery tickets against. It was relevant to my job, and while I certainly noticed the experience, I quickly chalked it up to just a curious happening and then forgot about it.

Later, it came to me that there was clearly a point to my being shown the winning lottery numbers the night before they were drawn: not for me to *win* the lottery (well, I could have if I'd purchased a ticket with those numbers, but I don't dwell on that). The point to me was to open the door of my awareness with a message of *Notice this … you've received some information in an unusual way, a premonition* (although I didn't associate that word with this lottery experience until years later, when my awareness deepened). Many awarenesses took quite awhile to come to me and sink in. These learnings came to me over time and were what I needed on some level after my NDE.

I strongly encourage people having intuitive experiences, or synchronicities (meaningful coincidences) to jot them down in a journal or notebook devoted to these experiences to remember them, start to see any patterns with the experiences over time, and integrate these experiences with your mind (thoughts) and body (as you may note how you feel when receiving intuitions).

During the weeks after the lottery number experience, I was into my new routine of simply working and being in the pottery studio (either for class or additional time practicing). As I finished a piece on the potter's wheel, I'd move it to the shared room for all the similar classes, where the wet clay could dry very slowly, which was far better than allowing it to dry quickly and crack in regular air. In this "damp room" (as it was called), the air was humidified to optimize the slow drying. In that room I felt like I was inside the earth, as there was such a rich, thick odor of clay and humid moisture. At first, it was odd to be in such an unusual space, but then it became a pleasure … like being instantly transported to a kind of tropical forest (a welcome relief to the snowy winter outside). Often, I'd see people in the damp room from other classes, as we all spent time there, carefully sliding our new creation onto a shelf without bumping someone else's clay masterpiece.

I was at the pottery studio a lot, and noticed a woman bustling in and out. After a few days, I struck up a conversation with Sarah there. She turned out to be a much more experienced potter than I … and would often share pointers with me on trimming or glazing my creations. We enjoyed chatting often and got to know each other better. One evening, I was reflecting about how many people were enjoying and benefiting from creating art at these local classes. As I drove home, my car tires crunching in the snow in the dark wintry night, I felt grateful to be alive.

In the following weeks, I started to get back with other new friends I had met in Kalamazoo. I knew it wasn't good to just hole up forever, as I had initially needed to do after my NDE. Since it was still difficult for me to be my old, gregarious self, I did a little visiting with new friends, but mostly worked at the TV station and went to the pottery studio, which was a perfect kind of meditation place … working in silence with the clay. Sarah and I started to hang out occasionally; she lived near me, was easy to be around, and I found it interesting talking with her.

One evening after I had been at the studio making cups from porcelain, which was so much smoother and slipperier from the rougher quality of the regular clay I'd been used to, I went home to bed. My head hit the pillow with a tired thud. That night, I had a very unusual dream. My handsome father was smiling broadly and greeting me; however, he looked like he was in his early twenties (the same age I was then). A striking quality of light beamed out of his blue eyes and entire face.

My father had died when I was 9 years old and he was 50, so to see him in this dream—13 years later—was such a treat. I was very aware of being "in" this lucid dream with him. He shared a poignant thought with me, and as he expressed it to me, I completely "heard" what he said. What was interesting to me as I reflected on this dream later was, his lips didn't move at all. He conveyed his message with a thought (mental telepathy), remarking about my being out on my own, after college, and working in my first job. He sent the thought to me clearly, "I'm so proud of you!"

This dream left me feeling wonderful and loved. When I awoke, I felt like I had really interacted with my father during the night. Enjoying the sensations, I did some errands during the morning and early afternoon then headed to the television station for my shift, which began at 3:00 p.m. I didn't think to share this dream with others, but was satisfied to cherish it on my own as it was very special to me.

As the seasons changed to spring then summer, I ventured out more and more over time after my NDE. I'd been invited to an event with my new friends in town. We were outside in the hot summer sun for hours; later, some of us went to a restaurant to cool off and grab a bite. Sarah was there, and I complained to her that I had a really bad headache (perhaps due to not drinking enough water while out in the hot sun most of the day). She motioned me to sit at another table with her saying "Don't tell anyone about this but I'm going to put my hands on your head. I want you to 'give' me the headache." I thought *What in the world is she talking about?!* But, my head was hurting so much, I was willing to try.

Sarah put her hands on my head. I glanced at our friends across the room and was happy no one was looking over at us, as I'm sure they'd think we were more than "out to lunch"! After a few minutes, Sarah leaned closer to my ear and said, sounding a little irritated, "You are *not giving me* the headache … concentrate on pushing it *out of your head*!" I closed my eyes and tried with great concentration to send the pain into her hands. After a few minutes, she exclaimed, "There! I've got it!" and started to move her hands up and down vigorously, like she was trying to shake something off.

I was bewildered by this whole thing, but thought to check in with myself. I did a quick scan and couldn't believe it. My headache was completely gone, and I felt great! I looked at her with great confusion, as if to ask *What did you just do?!* Sarah got my quizzical look and said in a hushed tone, "I'm a healer, but I don't want everyone to know about it … I'll explain some other time, but please don't tell anyone about this." I agreed and was so elated that I bounded off to join my friends on the dance floor and have a good time.

The next Saturday, Sarah and I were hanging out at her house. She was working on some home repairs. I helped her slather a coat of fresh paint on her walls. Our conversation turned to her spontaneous healing of my headache, as I had several questions. Sarah explained she had this ability to heal others' physical issues, but after people learned about it, they clamored for her help. It got to be too much, so she now kept her skill under wraps.

As we talked about her experiences healing others, Sarah mentioned a movie she liked, "Resurrection," starring Ellen Burstyn. I exclaimed that I'd enjoyed that movie too, as it was so interesting to watch a healer in action. Sarah was surprised I knew the film since it had come out about five years ago. She shared more about her metaphysical experiences—of physical healing and also intuitive experiences. I felt relieved as I listened to her, as if I could ask her about my recent unusual experiences. I described my recent vivid dream of my father and explained how it felt so real, and the genuine emotions I experienced. Sarah was familiar with this and said this was a real visitation from my father on the other side. It was a lot to digest for me. I knew nothing about spirits being able to visit or share a heartfelt message with their loved ones here on earth.

The idea of metaphysics was foreign to me, as I'd had little direct experience with intuitions, psychic ability, and the like when growing up. Now that Sarah had brought up this possibility, I started to remember a few experiences from my childhood. My mother seemed to have a sixth sense. There was one evening, shortly after I'd gotten my driver's license that I was driving home from the library. I took a right turn too sharply in our long boat of a station wagon. I hit the curb as I turned the corner (probably a little too quickly), and the back part of the station wagon car jostled back and forth and jumped up onto the curb, hitting a streetlight pole that was there. Much to my horror, it crunched that back right side of the car!

I drove home sheepishly, entered the house nonchalantly, and walked straight in to hang up the car keys down the front hall. Just as I did, I heard my mother call to me as she sat in the den. She said, deadpan, looking out at me in the front hallway, "You wrecked the car." I stopped in my tracks and turned to look at her, two rooms away. As we looked eye to eye, I said, "How did you know that?!" Somehow my mother got a hit—no pun intended—on what had happened (as we didn't have cell phones yet to report the news from the scene of the crime). I explained what actually happened and she came outside and was a little relieved it was more like a dent and scratch that the car being "wrecked", but I was amazed at her intuition at that moment!

There was another instance of intuition I recalled where my mom knew something was physically wrong with my sister in Minneapolis (who was trying to drive home for Mother's

Day to deliver a flat of lisianthus flowers to mom as a gift). Yet, my sister later reported by phone to mom that she had to turn back to go home because she had a scratched eye from her contact lens and it hurt so bad—though she was trying valiantly to continue to drive back to see mom and us—she could not continue with the five-hour drive. After hearing this update from my sister, mom told me about her intuitive knowing from early that morning before she received my sister's call confirming the reason why mom felt something was wrong.

After Sarah was so open to what I was saying about the vivid, real-seeming dream about my father who had passed away, I then told her about the winning lottery numbers in my dream. Sarah said something like, 'Kay, I think you may have changed a little after nearly dying that night.'

Her words swirled around in my head for days to come. Could they be true? As a healer, Sarah had seen many things I hadn't experienced (plus, she was older than me so had more life experience). She could more easily connect the dots between my NDE and these unusual experiences that had come through afterward in my sleep state, when I was relaxed. To me, it was a novel idea to consider that somehow I was now changed as a result of nearly dying, leaving my body, and then coming back in. Or, dying then being allowed to come back to live again.

Sarah was one of the first people that was perfectly placed on my path to help me with my new life after my near-death experience. I was so grateful I'd met her … and of all places … in a damp room full of wet pottery! This art class was certainly providing me with a lot more than glazed pots.

As I write this several years later, I was fact-checking the details on the movie "Resurrection" and was fascinated to read a plot summary that noted Ellen Burstyn's character, Edna, also went through a NDE. Edna later realized that she might have newfound hands-on healing abilities after talking with her Grandma Pearl, similar to the talk I had with Sarah. I've since learned from Kenneth Ring's work that some come back after a NDE with psychic or mediumistic abilities while others come back with the ability to heal with their hands.[3]

Having psychic abilities means knowing things about another person's life (or other information) via one or more extrasensory abilities such as: clairvoyance (or clear vision … from the French *clair* meaning clear, and *voyance* meaning vision), clairaudience (clear hearing), clairsentience (clear feeling or touching, which I liken to claircognizance … clear knowing), clairalience (clear smelling … I've also read about this called clairolfactory), and clairgustance (clear tasting). Mediumistic ability includes using these "clairs" to receive messages from people who have passed away (or crossed over … a spirit).

I've heard many mediums say that all mediums are psychic, but not all psychics are mediums. That is, mediums use the "clairs" above in bringing through messages from departed loved ones, where as psychics are more focused on bringing messages through about their client's life (such as their relationships, home life, job, etc.) While you can quickly find many references to these clair definitions online, one source described clairvoyance as "the ability to gain information

[3] from Kenneth Ring's and Evelyn Elsaesser Valarino's *Lessons from the Light: What we can learn from the near-death experience*, Moment Point Press, 1998, Needham, Massachusetts

about an object, person, location, or physical event through means other than the known human senses." (wikipedia.org).

Sarah helped me get the ball rolling, from a complete standstill where I was unaware. I was just trying to move forward in my life and starting to entertain the thought that something had shifted in me after leaving my body and coming back during the night of my NDE. As I write this now, I can clearly see how the NDE was the beginning of a completely new vector, or direction, in my life. If another person had told me about these experiences (dreaming the correct lottery numbers or having a real visit from a deceased father) after an NDE I might have been skeptical until they were clearly proven to me. In retrospect, I've become even more grateful to Sarah for her initial assessment and how it got my mental wheels turning with this possibility that I could later build upon.

I don't recall other direct earlier experiences with intuition in my life, other than the usual teenage experimentation with a Ouija game board with friends (which I don't recommend, by the way, as one can be opening to anything or anyone … definitely something you do not want to do)! Like other kids, I had the common fascination with telling ghost stories at sleepovers, or trying to create a cheesy little haunted house in the basement for friends to walk through on Halloween, but didn't have much other experience with the psychic or paranormal than that.

Oh, there was one other little thing. I recall wondering where babies came from when I was between age 6 and 10 or so, so I asked my sister. I could sense her not wanting to give me all the details, so I knew I would have to figure it out another way. Somehow, as I walked around our little city block in the sun, wondering this question … it changed to something more like, *Why are we here? What's the point of it all?* I remember the sun shining through the tree leaves in a beautiful shade of light green when the answer kind of came to me. I got it that I was here before and in a much different situation. It came to me clearly that I had been a black boy in the south without much, then I noticed how I was almost the opposite of that in this lifetime, as my family was very fortunate to be comfortable with respect to housing and food. I thought next, *Now, why would that happen?*

It occurred to me that one would learn very different things whether you had money or not, or the difference of what your experience was like based on what you looked like and where you grew up. So, as I continued with the questions and the answers just seemed to pop into my head, I came to know that reincarnation was what happened as a way for our soul to learn over lifetimes. At that moment, it made sense to me. Another idea that came which made sense to me at a young age, was that we had a kind of wrapper from lifetime to lifetime, but the essence inside was the same part learning more each time. Never mind that to my young self a metaphor of gum in a wrapper made sense to me at that time (as the wrapper can change, but you can't really get rid of gum … it just keeps changing forms). I sincerely hope that does not put anyone off. It's merely an example that made sense to a very young girl and what she was familiar with … gum.

I thought I had invented reincarnation that day! I was more than a little upset when I later learned that it was already a concept on the planet, and I hadn't invented it at all. But, it helped me with the grand scheme of things. Having this understanding that reincarnation made sense to me from a young age probably helped me later as more unfolded.

Chapter 3

Springboard to More Opportunities

In the first and second years after my NDE, I kept getting an inkling that I should move. Since college, I had this intuition that I would end up on one of the coasts. I came close, as I nearly entered a college curriculum that would have taken me to New York for one year of study (but my mom was not at all keen on me moving to New York). After college, I had a friend who had moved to San Francisco for work, so I decided to go visit her on my coveted one week of vacation. I had a total blast, visiting San Francisco for the first time, and thought back to a postcard of the Golden Gate Bridge a high school friend had sent me in Wisconsin years ago. During that high school timeframe, I was pretty enamored with that view and made a mental note that I would really like to see San Francisco someday. Well, my college friend had given me a launch pad for seeing that amazing bridge in person and so many other wonderful sights. After visiting her there, I had more than a little seedling of desire growing within me to return to California. So, I saved up for the next precious week of vacation in San Francisco, and after that fun second trip, it dawned on me. *Why am I saving up to spend just a few days a year there?! Why don't I just move there? After all, I've always envisioned myself living on one coast or the other.*

This wasn't an overnight decision. I started a pro and con list in my mind about whether this was a good idea or not. I'd made some wonderful friends in Kalamazoo that would be hard to leave, but *they could visit me and we could keep in touch* I thought. After my second trip to California, I came back to Kalamazoo and was determined to start preparing to move. Once I decide something, it can happen faster than expected. So, things around me seemed to hasten my journey and about two weeks before I was to drive cross-country to start my new life out west, I let my family in on what I'd been considering the last few years … a pretty big move.

"What? You're moving to California?!" I recalled some of my family members' responses were. I didn't quite understand why they were so surprised, as I had been thinking about this for quite some time now. In retrospect, I can easily see that I was not sharing my thoughts with them along the way, but rather, was quietly mulling this whole idea over internally. With that perspective, I could now understand their shock at my announcement.

I pretty quickly pared down my belongings, rented a trailer and hit the road. Since it was one of the hottest, most humid summers in recent years in Michigan, I couldn't even fly my beloved cat, Scooch, out to San Francisco to meet me when I'd arrived there. It had to be a certain, reasonable temperature outside for a pet to be flown in the baggage belly of the airplane. So, while the goodbyes to my close friends was so very hard, they truly wished me well, and one friend, who worked at a veterinarian clinic, kindly took care of Scooch for me until the cat could safely fly.

I was welcomed in San Francisco by friends I'd met through my college buddy. So by the evening of August 1st, I was a California resident, after living my entire life in the Midwest. After the huge inner change I'd experienced as a result of my accidental carbon monoxide poisoning, I'd now completed a huge outer change (though I didn't even think of it that way back then). Moving westward was like taking that last springy bounce off the end of a diving board. I had flown through the air and landed in a whole new swimming pool. While I'd met people in Michigan who helped me a great deal after my NDE, including Sarah and my other friends, the move to California opened up many possibilities to meet others who —I can now see as I write this—helped me on my journey beyond measure. I'm grateful—and very lucky—to add that my family was supportive of me both before and after this move.

PART II

RECOGNIZING DESTINY

CHAPTER 4

Nurturing Helpers

In the first several years in California, I was trying to set down roots like trying to find an immediate job and a place to live, then a job and a living space more suited to me longer-term, as well as widening my friendship circle. Being totally pre-occupied with these basic needs, everything else would have to take a back seat. As I got more settled, I didn't want to take any job that came along, but wanted to try and be purposeful about the type of job I hoped to get, so I worked with a wonderful career counselor in San Francisco that guided me along the process of determining more of what I wanted before I looked.

Looking at the kinds of things I was drawn to and what I liked to do, I honed in on a marketing or communications position but was also open to sales positions as well. This turned out to be time and money well spent, as despite the amount of effort it took to do the "homework" on all this, I landed a job that combined all of the above at a performing arts organization. I was thrilled and enjoyed working at it for many years.

About four or five years flew by in that job as I was focused on meeting new friends and more in San Francisco and after that time, though my marketing and sales job was moving along just fine, I kept yearning for something that would touch my heart a little more outside of work. I took a Myers-Briggs Type Indicator® one-day workshop and could see that counseling would be a good fit with my natural abilities (and who I was) as an appealing addition. So I brainstormed a few ideas to take one small step in that direction, then decided to work as a volunteer peer counselor with people who had acquired immune deficiency syndrome (AIDS). There was another option, to simply help those with HIV or AIDS with practical errands like shopping, but I was much more interested in trying to be of emotional support to them.

After being a volunteer at the non-profit on Wednesday evenings and meeting with one client for several months, I took on another role there, leading a support group on Tuesday evenings for other volunteers (the support group was mandatory for all peer counseling volunteers as it could be intense sitting with a person who was coming to grips with weighty issues and listening to their thoughts about the possible end of their life). I was really finding this volunteer work just what I had been looking for—so I also started to do the periodic weekend trainings to get new volunteers up to speed before taking on their first client. Plus, I still had my own client I saw weekly. Spending time with this dear man, and learning all he was going through physically and emotionally often left me closing the outer door to his house and walking to my car, thinking

... Now what in the world was I worried about in my little life? Working with him put everything into perspective, and I truly enjoyed our connection.

I liked my job, and the volunteer work was satisfying that part of me that wanted more connection or meaning. As I was yearning for that next step in my life, I decided to apply to get my master's degree in counseling and was thrilled to get into the California Institute of Integral Studies ("CIIS"), a school that was well-known for being academically rigorous. Their graduates had a high pass rate on the state licensing exams, but there was also a metaphysical elective curriculum that appealed to me. So it also offered really interesting courses that honored intuition above and beyond the important core of western psychology and academic ways of knowing.

An unexpected benefit to volunteering at the AIDS non-profit was meeting, and enjoying getting to know, other volunteers. Friendships developed over time and I found myself hanging out with a few of my new friends. One of my friends there was a guy named Randy who was a few years older than me. It was fun to talk with him as he was well-read and introduced me to subjects from counseling to metaphysical topics. After months of hanging out, Randy had gotten a work assignment that would take him to another state, halfway across the country, for three months. I offered to take him to the airport.

Before leaving the house to pick him up, I spontaneously grabbed a deck of cards. I thought ... maybe we'll be so early, we'll get bored and we could play cards. We were indeed early and chatted at his gate awaiting his boarding time. We'd already eaten and still had time to kill, so I put my hands in my jacket pocket and discovered the cards I'd completely forgotten about. I pulled them out and he playfully grabbed them out of my hands, fanning the deck out so only he could see them; then he selected one card that was hidden from my view and jokingly said, "Guess what card I picked?" I thought to myself, *Oh this is ridiculous ... but what the heck ... I'll play along.* I was going to say any old card that came to mind, but instead I closed my eyes and I first saw black. I decided it was not a heart or diamond. Next I saw spots, so I decided it must be a club and not a spade. Then, I saw nine splotches of black and said, "It's the nine of clubs." Randy's mouth fell open. "No way! It's the eight of clubs!" After a pause, looking at me intently, Randy asked, "How did you do that?!"

Honestly, I had no idea. At a much later date, I'd learn that I was using the extrasensory ability known as clairvoyance (clear vision). I was seeing the black, then the splotches that looked like circles in my mind's eye (or some call it, the third eye).

After Randy returned from his three-month work gig, we were at my house talking one evening. He was joking around about what else I knew besides coming so close to seeing clues (in my mind's eye) to that playing card at the airport. I could tell he'd be open to whatever I said, so I shared something a little unusual I'd been aware of for a few months.

Part of my graduate school training required me to work with a psychotherapist so I could learn more about what clients go through and how the therapist interacts with a client. It was like a type of apprenticeship, but an experiential one where you came to learn what clients experience. I joked with Randy, "Who are you supposed to know nothing about?" Randy said, "Who?" I replied, "Your therapist ... the time you spend with them is all about you, right? ... and you are not supposed to know about them." After that, I looked down as I shared with him that I felt I knew things about my therapist, Amy, that I had no rational way of cognitively knowing (even though I thought it might simply be my projections). Now Randy was curious and wanted to hear more. I told him details of Amy's interests when she was growing up, her high skill level in these interests, and her primary relationship. Randy took it all in neutrally, then observed, "You should check it out with her and see what's true." I immediately thought … *I could never do that!* That would be going beyond what's appropriate, and I didn't want to be intrusive.

I'll fast forward to my telling Amy about nearly intuiting the playing card. She asked what else had happened that I felt I intuited. I thought *I can't do this. It's too weird to know private information about someone. I should not do this.* But, she encouraged me to go ahead. My face got hot and a surge of adrenaline coursed through me, matching the level of fear I was feeling. I took a breath and haltingly began with the historical and personal information I knew about her.

After several minutes, she calmly said, "Would you like some feedback?" I thought, *How can she react as if this conversation is about the weather or the local football team?!* She must have had experience with intuition or psychic ability … I nodded yes, since she had kindly offered.

Amy went into detailed feedback on each point about her life, past and present. She then summarized. Everything I had said was true, with the exception of one small personal point. With my face still flushed from embarrassment that I'd surely crossed some personal boundary, I asked her, "Why is this happening?"

Amy's response included some explanations along with offering a few book recommendations so I could learn more about receiving psychic information. I ordered the books from a bookstore near work immediately. The next day at lunchtime, I zipped over to the Opera Plaza bookstore near the San Francisco Civic Center to pick up the books. The clerk at the checkout counter hastily stuck a bookmark inside the pages of the top book. Later that evening, when I was home chilling out, I opened up the Index to the main topic Amy was telling me about. The bookmark was stuck into the very page talking about that topic! This was yet another synchronicity (or meaningful coincidence) that told me I would benefit from reading this information. These synchronicities were getting my attention!

My therapist Amy was incredibly supportive about wanting to help me nurture this little seedling of psychic ability, as she called it. And, we *both* wanted to foster my practicing in other directions than knowing about her personally. I was all for that. Kindly, Amy even contacted someone well-versed in this field so that I could speak with her and learn more about what I was experiencing. Her referral was so helpful. What I was going through was evidently some kind of psychic opening. I started to read everything I could on the subject of intuition and psychic ability.

There were so many other interesting synchronicities and intuitions during this time. It's like my intuition and psychic abilities had been dormant for a few years as I dealt with starting my life in California. Now I was more settled. What allowed my intuitions and psychic abilities to flourish was: my noticing intuitions and testing them out to see if they materialized, the people who noticed my initial hints and their encouragement to share my stories of what was happening, and their validation and appropriate referrals. With their helpful input, I could purposely place myself in more of those right situations. I listened and learned as much as I could along the way, thanking those who were kind and supportive on my journey, from my desire to move to California, to the desire to volunteer, then to go back to school.

While this direction of my life was becoming clearer, the kind of information I was learning in graduate school would also prove invaluable—how to sit with clients, using both my thinking and intuition. It was refreshing to be at a school that honored intuition alongside the rigorous academic training. My own intuition seemed to grow stronger in this very practical environment. It was midway through my training at school that I needed to leave the performing arts marketing position I had so enjoyed in order to have enough time to do internships and classes.

As I write this, I can now see that in my work as a teacher to those who are noticing budding intuition, psychic, and mediumship abilities—I am now the one assisting others on their journey of development the same way that those early helpers assisted me. I'm aware now that my students come to me with many questions, just as they are becoming aware of their psychic mediumship abilities. It's enjoyable to be on the other side of the table, listening to their interesting stories of intuitions and psychic hits as I do my best to nurture their development. This process of helping the next generation of those with extrasensory or other abilities, reminds me of an extremely popular series of movies about learning magic from those who have experience with it.

As I was going through meeting people that helped me on my journey of psychic opening, I was reminded of a course I took while I was at the University of Wisconsin - Madison. My core curriculum was filled with required classes but I had a humanities elective to fill. I signed up for a course that dovetailed nicely and sounded like fun—folk (fairy) tales (including their history and how they came to be written). This course focused on the life and writing of Hans Christian Andersen; I am part Scandinavian, so this appealed to me. We were required to learn the five key elements of a good tale and then to write one ourselves.

So while I reflected back on taking this college course, several years later, I realized my life paralleled these key five elements: a lack, a journey, a test, helpers and/or opponents, and a resolution. After the process is completed, the tale may continue, with or without repetition of some or all of these elements. I was currently only to the "helpers and/or opponents part", but I was experiencing this pattern, nevertheless.

Years later, I became familiar with Joseph Campbell's work by watching a television special called "The Power of Myth" where Bill Moyers interviewed him as he discussed the hero's journey (similar to these key five elements listed above) and much other fascinating information. The hero's journey forms the basic template for many stories, books, modern television shows, and many (wildly popular) movies. In Campbell's book *The Hero with a Thousand Faces*, this journey is similar to what I learned in my class. It includes: the call to adventure, a supernatural aide or mentor, initiation by trials and adventures, victory, and return.

I recalled this folk tale class I took while in Madison, and the delightful teacher who brought the material to life with verve and a twinkle in his eye. Now I started to realize—after meeting Randy and Amy unexpectedly—that I might be on a journey of my own. I had my NDE. Then I started on an internal journey that was mirrored by my outward journey to California. Now I was meeting other helpers. It was simply my nature to ignore the opponents and move forward.

This model of a tale could likely apply to anyone's life. Right now, it helped me ground myself during a time when my world felt a little turned upside down with the rush of intuitive and synchronistic happenings. It's as if I didn't really get what happened in Michigan, though Sarah helped me get my wheels turning. Now I knew that I was different after my near-death experience. I couldn't get it at a younger age because I didn't have a framework to put it all into. I had no real exposure to intuition, psychic abilities, or premonitions. Now I was more fully able to accept that a pattern was emerging. Learning about these topics also helped me understand more about the language and experiences of this journey I was now on.

If you are experiencing synchronicities, intuitions or psychic knowings, you may relate to what I learned during this formative stage in my opening. You do not need to have had a NDE ... you may just be naturally intuitive ... so if you would like to integrate that intuitive part of yourself with your fabulous mind, heart, and body, I hope you can glean some helpful ideas from reading these stories of my unfolding and development.

Chapter 5

An Unexpected Visitor ... and Opening

In this chapter, I will share what people getting in touch with their mediumship abilities can experience before they fully understand what is happening or can put this kind of opening into context. That is, how bewildering it can be when you first encounter these kinds of experiences—out of the blue—with no previous knowledge of them. When I was first experiencing this, there were not several shows on television I could relate to or learn more from, as there are today (there were only one or two in the mediumship area that I stumbled upon, as I look back upon this time period). I wrote about these experiences (from a personal journal) in September after a trip from California to see my family in the Midwest one summer in the early 2000s. There, I wrote:

I feel like I'm having a second wave of psychic opening; the last wave was around 1992-93. Of course, I'm sure I receive messages and intuitions regularly, but on this trip, I really *got it* … that something new and unusual was happening to me.

I'd arrived in Madison, Wisconsin, and was staying at my brother, Greg's, place, since my sister's house—where we all congregated to visit—was already full with other visiting family. We were enjoying a really nice visit, and one evening before I went to bed, I noticed one book in a stack of books on Greg's coffee table. He was an avid reader, like many others in my family. The book really caught my eye for two reasons. First, I wondered why Greg would have a medium's book as I wasn't sure he really believed in this kind of thing. So, when I asked him about this he said he sometimes talked with a good friend of his about whether mediums were really connecting with deceased people or how that could happen.

Also, I was curious about this book by a medium (who could bring messages through from people who had passed away for their loved ones here) and I had just seen the medium, John Edward, on television just a few weeks before for the very first time. As it was the first time I had ever seen a medium work, I watched him give messages to people in the audience with detail. Not knowing how this could possibly work, I thought several things: *That isn't possible. What is he doing? How could he be doing that? How could that possibly work? My questions were not about this medium's skills, they were more about my wrapping my brain around this new information and trying to discern if it's something I could believe in at that moment.*

Though people in the audience seemed to be confirming what he was telling them, and even seemed delighted and relieved to get the information, I just couldn't understand how anyone could possibly get messages from dead people. I was a skeptic by nature, having never really thought about what happens after a person passes away as my young self saw death as kind of a black hole where not much was happening (despite my even earlier knowing that at some point we reincarnate). It wasn't all completely formed or cohesive, as I didn't think much about death and what comes next, if anything. That night, back at Greg's place, I read the medium's book a bit before falling asleep, tired from the busy day of visiting and running around with my young nephew and siblings.

The next night, my eight-year-old nephew asked me if I could stay at their house (my sister's house) that night. What are you going to say to an adorable child? Of course I wanted to … it was just a matter of logistical space available at her place, since she had others visiting. We worked it out so I could stay there at my sister's, and nephew's place, and since I was still about two hours jet-lagged—after all others had gone to sleep—I stayed up reading the medium's book Greg had given me.

I finished reading the rest of the book from my start the night before, and then I dove into reading the exercises at the back of the book (before I fell asleep) on how to develop your psychic and mediumship abilities. Word to the wise: while I thought I was simply *reading* these exercises, I was actually "doing" them … as I learned after the events of this evening.

I was so inexperienced in anything from this realm. I was reading exercises about raising your vibration (and how to do it), and the like. As I drifted off to sleep that night … little did I know that I had opened myself up to the world of spirit people who had passed away. As I was in that hazy state between being awake and being asleep, a sea of images came flooding forth in my mind's eye. I saw an image of a man who was looking at me and telling me what had happened to him as he passed away, in intricate detail. I didn't know who he was, or who the message was for—at this initial juncture of my seeing a spirit person—but I could see what he was showing me … and it wasn't at all rosy.

I saw a young man. He had a gunshot wound to his stomach and the blood showed through his white, short-sleeved shirt that had a little pattern on it. He was not clean-shaven—he had two to three day stubble on his face. If the truth be told, he looked grizzled and pretty sketchy. I was kind of afraid of him … and he was *right in front of me!* I saw him so vividly … as if he was two feet from my face … and he was! At this point, I was inexperienced in receiving people in spirit. Seeing this man with blood all over him and not knowing who he was or what he wanted freaked me out.

I was just starting to see spirit people after reading a book, and I did what some people might do after such an unsettling and unexpected experience. I quickly got physically ill (not to be too graphic, but I threw up all night long). The night was also further punctuated by a rousing thunder and lightning storm as well, which made it all the more surreal. I know I call another chapter "a dark and stormy night" but this really was one, indeed! What's more, this was all happening before I knew what was going on, and I was not in my home, but visiting at my sister's. I felt so comfortable there, but didn't know what was happening so just had to tell myself I had the flu and needed to get better (sound familiar … as in Chapter 1?).

That night, it felt like a dam broke and there was a flood of new and different kinds of images flooding forth into my mind—later I'd learn they weren't just images, but spirit people coming to speak to me. Somehow, seeing that medium on television, then reading this book, kick started a whole new chapter in my life!

I note that when I feel ill, I am more open and my feelings are more noticeable. So perhaps I needed no distractions to just sit and read this book, and make some space for what was about to arise … but there I was, feeling and experiencing it all.

The next day I was recovering in my sister's bedroom as she invited me to go up there and get some rest. I slept and rested most of the day, sipping water and trying to get back to normal, as I had to fly out to San Francisco the next day. After the morning and afternoon all cooped up, I got stir crazy and wanted to get up to take a shower and then a brief walk in the warm, summer air.

My eight-year-old nephew, getting wind that I was finally emerging from my cocoon, insisted on joining me. So, we walked … very slowly … around their lovely neighborhood. He was sweet, jumping around, and talking with me—keeping me company—as I re-entered the world. I had to kind of inwardly chuckle as he said to me near the end of our walk, what I'm sure he heard my mother or sisters say a few hours earlier, "Kay-Kay, you've always had a sensible stomach." I'm sure my mom or sisters said "sensitive," but it was adorable when he said that as we finished our little walk in the summer sunshine. I adored him, before and after that comment, as he just had this way of sharing his view of things that was creative and unique (not to mention how he's invented some pretty descriptive words).

On the airplane home, I wondered after that unexpected spirit came through to me that weekend; *could I do what these mediums do?* Then, I thought *Maybe I don't have to know what is happening with all this right now.* Even after that night, I never could place that man with the gunshot wound to his torso that disturbed me so (even though he wanted to be seen and somehow could see, that even in those early days ... I had abilities to perceive him). That night, as I unwittingly opened to see that person who had died a violent death ... I had opened to the spirit world by doing those exercises in the book before I knew anything about getting grounded, protecting oneself, or only opening to the spirit people who are your clients that you are reading for. I knew nothing of these important basics then.

At that time, what I could glean from this was: maybe there was something to these 'messages from people who had passed away' business, and I seemed to need to know that I had this ability. Clearly, there was more I needed to learn (judging from the disturbing results of that night), but the dots were starting to line up ... even if they weren't yet quite connected for me.

The Kicker

As I wrote these notes in my journal on white lined paper with a black felt pen while still on that airplane ride back to my home in California, it helped me to try to make sense of this unsettling spirit visit I had back in Wisconsin. Then, when I got off the airplane in San Francisco and walked through the SFO airport toward the entrance, I heard something surprising. As I walked hurriedly toward the outer doors at the airport, eager to get home to my own bed to sleep, I heard over the intercom, "John Edward to the white courtesy telephone.

John Edward to the white courtesy telephone." I stopped in my tracks! *What?!* I thought, stunned, *Did I just hear that?* Then, I heard it again blaring over the intercom so all could hear it.

If anyone needed a sign that said, *NOTICE THIS EXPERIENCE* … there it was. Regardless of whether that might be a common name, it caught my attention and made sense with several experiences I was having. I was to notice this mediumship world and connect the dots between seeing the television show a few weeks ago, reading the book from my brother, seeing a spirit person myself vividly, and hearing this medium's name. You've heard the phrase, the third time's a charm … so here were *four* events to catch my attention. I walked out of the SFO airport in a daze from that final synchronicity, but also with a smile on my face and a twinkle in my eye. I was getting that the spirit world could create some meaningful coincidences to catch your attention, if you cared to notice. What's more, it seemed they had a heck of a sense of humor, to boot, using this fourth way to get me to notice the world of mediumship. Believe me … I noticed!

Chapter 6

James Van Praagh Workshop: Message from the Other Side

I saw that world-renowned medium James Van Praagh was coming to San Francisco to offer a one-day workshop on developing your psychic and mediumship abilities. Given the unusual experiences I was having, I thought I could benefit from attending, to learn some exercises to develop. The day was mainly outlined as lecture and some exercises, but I secretly hoped that James Van Praagh would offer to give a few messages from people in spirit for this student audience. If he did, I hoped to hear from my father, Roy, who had crossed over when I was young.

It was a clear San Francisco morning the day I attended Mr. Van Praagh's workshop. What a treat to be up on Nob Hill, since I was rarely in that part of the city. I entered the Masonic

Auditorium filled with anticipation—armed with my spiral notebook to write down whatever might help me with my ongoing development. James Van Praagh came on-stage and started to share an introduction to this metaphysical realm. I literally wrote as fast as I could, trying to capture everything he said.

My coursework at my graduate school, CIIS, complete with exposure to many metaphysical concepts from reading, helped prepare me to take in James' wonderful introduction. After hearing James speak for nearly an hour, I loved all he was saying. When he finished, I realized it was information I already felt to be true. This made me reflect that perhaps I was further along in this journey than I thought … or was in the right place to learn more at the very least. It was a nice moment, just to notice that I was in the right ballpark. It felt good to realize I was so in tune with such a like-minded person who was gifted in the mediumship world.

The morning progressed with an exercise where we were to tune in and receive a message from someone in spirit (a person who had passed away to the other side) that we knew. Of course, I was concentrating hard on receiving a message from my dad. As I did, in my mind's eye (also called the third eye) I saw something surprising. My first and only dog, Brandy, was running around and wagging her tail energetically! I loved my Brandy so much; she'd been in spirit since I was in college. So it was a delight to see her howling a "hello!" as she did when she was very excited to see someone.

I feel badly now that I almost kind of shushed her away. After all, I was going about the serious business of trying to hear from my long-lost father! But my beloved Brandy kept running around me like crazy. I finally gave in and simply enjoyed seeing her again. As a quick flashback, I so badly wanted a dog for a pet as a young girl. But at first, my family thought I might be satisfied with a goldfish instead. My eight-year-old self thought, you can't play with a goldfish, or walk a goldfish! So, I persisted in asking for a dog. I can't recall how it all happened, but finally I was taken by our sweet neighbor, a man who was a board member of the local humane society, to the animal shelter to pick out a real dog! He helped me both choose, and name, my first dog ever—Brandy. I was so happy to have her, and my whole family fell in love with Brandy. This moment at a workshop became very special. It kind of made me laugh, to get my dog instead of my dad.

James led us in an exercise where we tried to read for each other, using some helpful psychometry techniques. Psychometry is using the energy that is kind of imprinted upon an object used often by its owner (such as a watch or keys) to more easily give them a reading. Then it was time to break for lunch.

Given my recent experiences of seeing people, as I was just beginning to fall asleep, I had a burning question to ask Mr. Van Praagh. I was not sure if he'd answer, but I had to try. So I raced up to the stage before he left for the lunch break. Several of us were standing near the stage, and James graciously came up to speak with us. I patiently waited. Finally James looked at me, and I told him, "I am seeing people just before I fall asleep …" Before I could say more, James said, "Yes, you are." This shocked me a bit as I thought to myself *How did he know that?!,* but I pressed on, not wanting to take up his precious time.

I continued, "What do you think is happening?" To this, he replied, "You are probably a medium." I was floored! World-renowned James Van Praagh just told me I was likely a medium! *What?* I thought to myself. I asked him next who I could study with privately in Northern California. He suggested I go to the local Spiritualist Church to see if they offered ongoing teaching classes (also known as a development circle). I said, "Thank you, sir," and he playfully responded, "You are welcome, Ma'am."

Honestly, I don't recall how I got down the steep hill to the Korean barbecue place for lunch. Perhaps I floated down the hill … being in a bit of a daze from this interchange with James Van Praagh. As I ate my barbecued chicken and rice while sipping a lemon-lime soda, I looked out onto the street and tried to process what I had just heard: "… probably a medium …" Hearing this helped me to validate the foundational experiences I'd had in the psychic and premonition arenas since my near-death experience years ago, but if I really was a medium, what would that mean in my life? How was everything going to change … again?

Back in class again, James continued teaching, answering questions, and leading us through more exercises. Then, about 45 minutes before the end of the event, James asked, "Would you like me to give some messages?" The 300-person audience roared a collective, "YES!" James began to give messages to selected audience members. There seemed to be a theme, from husbands to their wives. I relaxed, as James shared that he can feel when audience members are thinking, "Please come to me with a message … please!" The message-receiving, I learned that day, seemed to work better if one was neutral, and did not have their legs or arms crossed. So I sat there, very la-dee-dah nonchalantly. After about three messages with emotions ranging from love to regret or remorse, my ears perked up at the next introduction.

James looked at the approximately 100 seats in our section of the Masonic Auditorium main floor, waved in our direction and said, "Did someone over here lose a collie dog?" (My late pup, Brandy, was a collie.) I was sure that several people would respond affirmatively, so I didn't bother raising my hand (and since I was initially sure the message was not for me, I didn't bother to turn and look at the people behind me to see if it was their message, as I was in the front row). James continued, "This collie was smaller than most, and some people didn't like that … the dog is telling me that made her feel bad." James went on to discuss a certain health condition this collie had. I could no longer ignore all these accurate facts and sheepishly raised my hand. James requested, "Could you stand up, please?" Just then, a runner raced over and handed me a cordless microphone. The adrenaline shot through my body—as it would have if I'd been in an Olympic event at that moment! My legs were shaky as I tried to stand.

James gave me a full-blown message from my wonderful, one-and-only dog Brandy (that had come to me earlier in the day). I blurted out, "I saw her this morning during the exercise you led!" and James responded, "Well, she's running all around you and in the aisles … Oh, she's just jumped up and put her front paws on you!" The audience emitted a collective, "Awww …" I was in a daze, listening and trying to give "yes" or "no" feedback (as requested). He even said that before we got her from the dog pound, when she was nine months old, she had been malnourished and abused by her previous owner. After these evidential (or provable) details showing that it was really Brandy, Mr. Van Praagh shared the main message for me: "Your dog wants to say, thank you for being my healer." Brandy was so appreciative of all the love and caring my huge family of nine had provided her.

Then, James shared a tidbit, from a dog's point of view as Brandy said, "… and thank you for not putting curtains on the windows next to the front door so I could look out and see who was walking by." I thought, that's an odd message, but it made sense, because barking at the pesky mailman (and others) was a big priority for Brandy!

I summoned up my courage to call my family to share this message. After all, they didn't know I was exploring this subject. My brother answered and after we exchanged greetings, I explained I was at a class with James Van Praagh, the well-known medium and author, partly to try to get a message from our dad. My brother relayed that to other family members with him in the kitchen area of the house we grew up in, then he waited to hear what was next.

When I said next the message I received was not from dad, but from our dog, Brandy, my brother quickly had to hand the phone to someone else (as I think hearing this unexpectedly may have struck an emotional chord because we all so dearly loved this wonderful dog of ours). As I shared tidbits of the messages from Brandy, the phone got passed around from one person to another. It can be a little odd to be mid-sentence, then all of a sudden, hear a new person's voice on the line. So, over the years, I'd ask them to at least say they were passing the phone along before they did it suddenly. Now sometimes they would say first, “Here’s a ‘hand over’!” as they knew I preferred this heads up instead. This day, however, that “hand-over heads-up” went right out the window. This, I knew, was an unusual phone call.

About the third or fourth person who was handed the phone was my mother, and she got emotional, too when she heard that Brandy had come to visit via a world-renowned medium, recalling a memory of us trying to fit five people into a station wagon with all our luggage and coolers and gear to get from our cottage to home. She said through her tears, “Poor Brandy only had about one square foot to sit in between all our stuff …” as she quickly passed the phone to someone else. My initial thought was they might think I was a little loopy calling with this news, but it really brought our loving memories of Brandy to the surface.

What a day! I was forever changed, and I learned first-hand that pets can share their thoughts and feelings through a medium (as this accurate and loving message went on for 10 to 15 minutes). In addition to the great practice I got with my psychic and mediumship skills—and confirmation of my budding mediumship—it was well worth the price of admission!

Chapter 7

A Dark and Stormy Night

In the early days when my psychic and premonition experiences after I nearly died turned to something entirely different—the mediumship—I didn't often realize what was happening as the messages started to come in. It was a little like being in a regular dream then you start to realize that it's a lucid dream ... or it's a dream where you feel like a loved one is really visiting you in the dream ... it kind of sneaks up upon you before you realize what's happening. If you haven't had these experiences, perhaps you can relate to having an intuitive feeling or know something is about to happen, and then it does! Or, you feel like you can sense the presence of a departed loved one or friend during your waking state. Or, maybe you notice a synchronicity, a meaningful coincidence. I now started to be open to all kinds of synchronicities or unusual extrasensory experiences; as they were proving to make life a lot more interesting and fun.

One of the earlier spontaneous messages that came to me occurred as I was just emerging from sleep one morning. In those first few moments of not being quite asleep and not yet fully awake, I felt like I was daydreaming and it appeared just like a film or video in my mind's eye. I saw a friend from junior high and high school. I saw her dressed in black, on a stage, playing her cello with a chamber orchestra. She played masterfully … engrossed in what she was doing, while I watched.

I thought to myself, "Hmmm … I wonder why I'm thinking of that." I know Sue to be a wonderful person, but we weren't really in touch over the years after high school, so I was curious about seeing this as it was so out of the blue. I shrugged it off and turned on the hot water in the shower. I would not usually describe my personal bathing habits here, but there's a point to including this detail.

Other thoughts came in. I didn't really pay attention to them until it became startlingly clear that these were not my thoughts. They were someone else's and conveyed information to me in little bits.

A man who identified himself as a music teacher was talking to me, through his thoughts, and I was receiving them, whether I wanted to or not … I wasn't even fully aware of what was happening. He said his last name to me. This all came to me clairsentiently as I felt it, and clairaudiently as I heard it (not out loud but inside my mind, as you might remind yourself to pick up eggs at the grocery store).

He continued to convey messages to me from his thoughts to mine. At one point in my disbelief, I stopped him and asked, "How do I know this is real?" Honestly, I'd never heard voices before! I asked again, "How do I know you are real and conveying messages I should pay attention to?" His personality came through loud and clear as he became a little irritated at my questions. I had been shaving my leg, which was propped up on the wall in the narrow shower stall. Just as he was answering with a raised voice and quickened tone—sounding pretty frustrated with me—my leg slipped down the shower wall and my foot slapped the ground on the wet tiles, creating a splash. Now, he really had my attention!

He said with a raised voice, emphatically, "My family came from Belgium and my wife's name was ____________!" He told me his wife's name as well (omitted for privacy). These were facts I could ostensibly look up, as proof of who he was. I thought back to him, in this silent conversation, "Well, OK then, why are you telling me all this?"

He said, "I want you to pass this message along to Sue." I replied in thought to him, "She'll think I'm crazy … no way." He was upset again with me. Then, I gave in and said to him in thought, "All right, all right … I will get her phone number from another mutual friend and pass your messages along." He said, "Good, now here's the main message for her." And, I thought … *what? That was all just a prelude?*

Then he said, with tenderness and great sincerity: "Please tell Sue that she was the BEST student I EVER had."

Again, I promised him I would. Now, I had gone and done it; I was on the hook to follow through. As I dried my hair, I thought of the enormity of his words. Here was a man I'd never heard of, but clearly, he had been a music teacher in the school system in my hometown for decades. Think about how many hundreds of students he must have taught at school in his long career … let alone how many private students. The message he wanted to pass along seemed important to a man who had spent his entire career probably listening to a lot of squeaky notes from so-so students over the decades of his life's work.

Sue was the BEST student he EVER had.

I now understood how this could be important to his legacy. After he had reviewed his life, his impact on such a talented student became more evident. Sue's musical excellence from such an early age, was evident, and here he was, showing her to me on a professional orchestral stage! Honestly, I didn't know anything about Sue's life … let alone if she ever performed on stage or even still played the cello!

After a few days regrouping, I got up the nerve to call a mutual friend and ask for Sue's phone number. Then I had to get up the nerve to call Sue and risk sounding like a fruit loop. But, I had promised this man. So I swallowed my pride and called as I flopped down on pillows in front of the gas fireplace, the only source of heat in my flat during the bone-chillingly cold San Francisco winter.

Sue picked up the phone. *Oh no!*, I thought, *Now, I really have to relay all this!* "Hello?" I thought, *oh gosh, now I have to actually say this* … so I looked down at the notes I had taken, trying to be as deferential as possible, as I didn't want to freak her out. I started with, "Hi, Sue, this is Kay Fahlstrom … remember me from high school? Well, I got your number from Rita and—well, you may not believe in this stuff, but I am a medium who can receive messages from people who have passed away, and I got a message for you. Would you like to hear it?" She replied something to the effect that she wasn't quite sure if she believed in this kind of thing, but she was willing to hear the message.

I gave the initial details about this man and his career and connection with her (as I did not know who he was myself). I asked Sue if she knew he had passed away and I also asked if she knew his nationality. She thought he was Belgian, as he had told me (again, this country detail has been changed for privacy). When I shared his main heartfelt message for her, she took it in for a few beats and then said something humorous. This music teacher also taught a few of her siblings … so it was a big deal that she was his most talented (in light of her siblings probably being excellent as well, I surmised). And, she was his best student ever, even beyond the hundreds of other kids he taught over the decades.

Sue and I continued talking for a bit. I said it was OK if she didn't believe in this, but I had felt compelled to follow through. Our call ended, and it felt a bit awkward (understatement), but I'd done my duty to that man who had passed away … that man who was now in spirit. And, I am quite sure Sue had a great story for her husband that night at the dinner table!

Encore

As an encore to this performance above, I thought I'd share about a visit to my family a few years later, in fall 2005. As I learned from Sue that this man was indeed a music teacher in our home town, I now conveniently had an easy way to check some of the identifying details he shared in his messages. During my family visit, my sister wanted to go to the Green Bay Public Library to return and pick up new items, so I snuck away to do some research on this man who had come through to me unexpectedly. A very helpful reference librarian predicted I'd probably find nothing, but I pressed on, as I hoped to at least find his obituary to see if there were any hints to his nationality.

While I typed search words into the electronic library catalog, the librarian was searching local records and doing an Internet search on this teacher. She found a local record listing the teacher's birthday, and the month and year of his death, so I could then search that month in microfiche of the *Green Bay Press Gazette* newspaper for his obituary. She also found several items on the Internet. One was a website created by someone in their immediate family. And there it was. The family was indeed from Belgium (this identifying detail is changed from the actual country for privacy … though the small countries' populations are very similar). This nationality was a fact proudly displayed on their website. I checked some of the other details of the message and they fit.

This heartfelt message from my hometown music teacher reached his favorite talented student. Why did he come through to me? Because I knew Sue. Even though we had never been in touch after high school … he knew I was a medium who could get in touch with her (via mutual friends) in hopes of passing his messages along. I promised I would, and I did. This was the start of many future messages where I became used to people thinking I was a little out there. But instead of worrying about that possible ridicule, I felt compelled to carry out the sincere wishes of these people in spirit. In fact, there were thousands of messages that I would pass along to people who had varying degrees of belief in mediums.

As I started to confirm provable facts from messages of people who had passed away (or died), I began to prefer the term, "crossed over" instead of both prior descriptions. I came to learn those in spirit are not dead at all, but are simply crossed over to the other side of the veil and still have their consciousness complete with their mind, memories and emotions all intact. They simply don't have that physical body any longer as it ceased to function.

Why Me? Receiving an Actor's Message

As I noted above, when I started to receive messages from spirits on the other side, I noticed that they often started with a kind of video or film-like sequence that played in my mind's eye. I received this clairvoyant imagery to—I later realized—know who the message was for or about. So, back in the early days of my receiving mediumistic messages from spirit people, sometimes I had to first get into the message before I even realized it was a message (and not just me daydreaming or thinking).

I also find it fascinating that these early messages in this chapter were received when I was in water. Yes, you read that correctly. In the prior message—as you read—I was literally in the shower. In the message that follows, my hands were deep in hot water as I did the dishes at the kitchen sink … anxious to get out of town for a week-long holiday up to the restorative woodsy Russian River recreation area in Northern California. As I noticed this, I thought back to the old dark and stormy nights depicted in movies about people having séances to contact the dead. I always thought that was a cheesy dramatization to make a movie seem a little spookier as the lightning and thunder crashed and boomed!

In these early days, I internally joked with myself that perhaps I'll have to be a medium who gives messages from sitting in a hot tub, or have to sign on as a cruise ship medium … if water seemed to help. While this was just a joke to myself, I wondered about the connection to water and how it may have made receiving my first few messages easier.

Since I was starting day one of a week-long vacation, I am quite sure my mind was more open, not thinking about rushing to work on time or the stresses of the full-time job I enjoyed at a large financial services company, where I worked in the marketing department, writing and editing newsletters and brochures for clients.

As my mind drifted while I was doing dishes at the sink, I started to see, in my mind's eye, a video play out. It initially felt like a memory, but it was so vivid and detailed as I saw a well-known television ("TV") actor come out on stage in a tuxedo. I remembered the sit-com TV show he was on and I'd watched it multiple times while growing up. This actor began a moving tribute to a deceased actor who was his friend and colleague (who was also a well-known actor). I vaguely registered the thought … *Hmm, I wonder why I'm thinking about the Academy Awards show I already saw?*

As I continued to wash dishes, I started to hear, clairaudiently, a song from the 1950s, I believe (one that described, in its lyrics, a captivating female). While hearing this song, I recognized the melody and lyrics to it as I knew them by heart (as my older siblings had records from this era). I started to then clairsentiently know this message was for his wife or daughter. This knowing then jarred me out of my hazy, relaxed state. I thought to myself, "Wait! Whose daughter?!" Then, I realized what was happening and the content of the message started to flow faster, I thought, *Oh my gosh, this is a message from a SPIRIT person!*

I raced across the length of my kitchen and living room over to my desk on the far side of the flat to grab a notebook and pen. As I ran back to the kitchen table, my hands still dripping wet from washing dishes, I sat down. Now understanding that this was a message from a spirit person, I looked up and said, "OK, I'm ready … what do you want to say?" I scribbled down some messages, including three names he said connected to him along with messages for his wife, children, and family. The messages were short and sweet and clear as could be.

I was stunned. I thought, *why in the world would this actor want to come to me?* I was living all the way up here in San Francisco. Surely, I thought, there were many talented mediums in Los Angeles (or wherever he lived) that he could come through to with his messages. For some reason, he chose me that day (maybe because I knew *all* the lyrics and melody for that exact old song he came through with … who knows?). Just for the record, I was not some kind of crazed fan, either. I never seemed to be like others who really hoped to meet a famous person one day. I had a prior co-worker at the performing arts organization that would say, "They put their pants on one leg at a time, just like the rest of us, right?" as if to say, in her own way … we are all alike (famous or not). So while I could appreciate how talented famous people can be, I just wasn't a person craving to meet actors or politicians or sports people.

I diligently wrote this actor's messages until they stopped. Then, I tried to double check by asking if there were any other messages he wanted to say to his loved ones. Nothing. He was done sharing his messages. So, the notebook with this actor's messages was put aside, and I threw my suitcase in the car. I was off on my long-awaited vacation at last!

When I returned home and came across those message notes, I thought … I'd made an unofficial promise of sorts to spirits that came through to me that I would try to pass messages along to the recipients, especially after all the effort and energy it took them to come through to me! Trying to do so, I did some research on his family on the Internet to see if I could get any kind of contact information for his wife. (Yes! By this time in my story, the Internet finally existed so I could look things up!) This turned up nothing, so I let it go.

Some time went by then I had a flash of intuition. Well … if I could get up my courage to call my prior colleague at the arts organization (that I worked at for years)—who was in charge of booking the talented performers—I might get some sort of lead on the agent for this actor in spirit so I could pass along his messages to his family. Why was I even thinking this? Because I had promised the music teacher man earlier in this chapter that I would try to pass along messages to the intended recipients wherever possible. It was a kind of pact that I was trying to follow through on.

Trying to get the actor's messages through, I tried to shelve my feelings of being "out there" and left a message for Tom at the performing arts organization. I felt more than a little awkward, "Err … Tom, this is Kay Fahlstrom … I used to work there for years. Well, you may think this is a bit out there, but I'm also a medium after a near-death experience and I just received a message from … (and I named the late actor). Do you happen to know who his agent was so I could pass the messages along to his widow?" I could just imagine Tom's face as he listened to this message. Honestly, I was not holding my breath about getting a call back from him.

A day or two later, I got a call from Tom's assistant with the actor's agent and contact information. I was grateful for this information so I could simply pass along this actor's message. I next got the email address of the agent from the receptionist there, and emailed these detailed messages from the actor to the agent asking them if they would please pass them on to his widow.

As time went by, I wasn't sure if the messages from this actor were ever sent to his wife via the agent, so I simply let it go. This sometimes happens to mediums as you try your best to pass along a message from a spirit person—but sometimes messages do not land despite your best efforts.

Many months later (long after I'd forgotten this experience), I was driving to work one morning, excited to be meeting a friend that night for a film festival. I was happy to have something to look forward to after work. As I was flipping around from song to song on the radio as I drove closer to the Golden Gate Bridge, I stopped to listen to a snippet of an interview. I don't usually do that as I prefer to sing along with songs as I'm zipping into work.

The disc jockey was interviewing someone who was in town for some reason. I listened and listened, wondering, *Who are they talking with?!* as they did not say throughout the interview. Finally, near the very end of the interview the DJ revealed he had been talking with the late actor's (the same man that had come to me with messages) son. And I already had tickets (for weeks now) to see his new movie that night. Coincidence? You decide.

A little discombobulated from that synchronicity, I worked away that day. The thought occurred, did the late actor's message ever get from the agent's email Inbox to his widow? I wondered if she never received it as this new synchronicity played out. I didn't know, but how strange that I'd be in the same theater with his son. Before the movie began, an emcee stated that you could come meet the actors after the show near the stage. As we watched his son's movie that evening, another thought crossed my mind *Am I supposed to try and meet his son now?* I was not a groupie at all. Wow. This medium thing was not for the faint of heart. Quickly after that thought, my willingness resurfaced vibrantly as I was truly willing to be of service, though sometimes it was a little difficult (a small price to pay in order to help those in spirit who were trying so hard to pass along a message or two).

I enjoyed the film with my friend. His son was introduced as part of the cast after the show, and I quickly said to my friend before our late dinner, "Can you please wait out front for me … I have to do something." She looked at me, like, "Huh?" and I zoomed off … not knowing whether I'd be able to pass along the message tonight.

I waited as people tried to speak with the young actor. When I did have my chance to talk with him, I tried to be very gentle as I broached the topic. First, I started by explaining that I am a medium and I got a message from his father, and would he like me to tell it to him then or another time? Well understandably, he was not quite expecting this, as he probably expected just to chat with fans. He looked pretty startled then said he would like to hear the messages. I gave him my card and suggested he call me the next day or later in the week … as I was quite sure this party like atmosphere wasn't really the time or place. For whatever reason, I never got a call from him. Perhaps he lost my card, or maybe I was one of many cards women gave him that night (though I'm sure I was the only one that was a medium and not interested in other connections than passing along his dad's messages). I completely respect that he didn't call. After all, it was an unusual experience he had, meeting me, and I'm sure this evening was a fun blur to him. So, if the late actor was still trying to get his message through to the whole family through his son, he lined all these details perfectly. But I'm sorry to say it didn't work.

As an afterthought, many years went by and my mediumship messages and clientele developed (where it was usually very easy to get ALL the messages through directly to my clients). Going through old files, I came across the actor's messages from those years ago. It dawned on me that I never did check to see if any of the names he said made any sense to his actual life.

Just out of sheer curiosity, I looked up the three names I received from this late actor way back when in a quick Internet search. As I looked up each one, I wrote on a notebook what I'd found out. No one was more surprised to me to find that each name he gave me was that of a very close family member!

While initially befuddled why a well-known actor would come through to me, a medium in Northern California, I eventually came to realize that anyone in spirit can come to any medium they choose. What's more, perhaps this connection was made because this departed actor knew I was going to meet his son at that event so I could easily try to pass along his messages to his family. I'm not sure (to this day) that the messages ever reached his family.

Chapter 8

James Van Praagh Sent Me: Skeptic Turned Believer

If you are at all skeptical about mediumship, you may relate to some of my thoughts in this chapter.

In the earlier chapter, when I asked James Van Praagh who I might study mediumship with locally, he suggested I try the local Spiritualist Church to find out whether they offered a development circle for people interested in improving their mediumship abilities. As I noted earlier, when I'd first seen a medium on television, I was skeptical. My left brain couldn't quite comprehend how it was possible to receive messages from the other side. By now, I'd not only seen James Van Praagh give evidential messages to others, but I had received a lengthy message from Mr. Van Praagh that was detailed and accurate. And, I'd received those few messages described earlier, but I still wasn't completely convinced so I needed *even more* information.

So off to the local Spiritualist Church I went. Prior to the Wednesday evening service, a hands-on healing was offered. I checked it out first from the larger congregation room. As I watched people go into the smaller, cozy, den-like room to the side where the healings were occurring, I noticed that people sat in an empty chair. A Church representative greeted the new person then put his or her hands near the participant's head. As people left the room, they thanked him or her and seemed lighter, happier, and more relaxed. I thought, *Well, this can't be all bad ... I'll give it a shot.* I noticed which healer's energy I was more drawn to, and wondered how their intention might affect this experience. I received the healing experience, which was pleasant.

After the healing portion of the evening, but before the service began, a Church representative said to me, "I haven't seen you here before, have I? How did you find us?" I replied, "No, this is my first time here," adding, "James Van Praagh sent me."

Well! He turned stark white, his eyes opened wide in surprise, and his body jerked backward a little as he stammered, "JAMES VAN PRAAGH?!" I didn't realize I'd cause a stir with that detail. I knew Mr. Van Praagh was a well-known medium and author, and this reaction confirmed that. I explained how I was at his workshop and asked for a place where I could find further classes, so Van Praagh suggested I see if any development circles were being offered at the church. The man said I could learn more about this in the program and from the announcements tonight.

After this first evening at the Spiritualist Church, I went back several times for both their Wednesday evening and

Sunday morning services, which often included messages from an audience's member's departed loved one via a medium. At this time, I was still checking all this out—how a medium started a message, was the message uplifting or helpful, and how did the recipient react? It's my nature to check something out thoroughly before I form an opinion.

I attended the church regularly now and started to receive a few messages from various mediums. I'd take notes, so when a message seemed to be evidential (or provable), I often would share it with my family members back east as sometimes I did not know information that was coming through firsthand. For example, when a spirit message came through from an uncle on my mom's side of the family, I didn't know if it was accurate (as he had lived in a faraway state so I didn't have all the historical details).

When I first told one of my sisters on the phone that I was going to church on a Wednesday night, her reaction was alarm, "Are you ill or something?!" I understood her surprise, chuckled, and explained that, after I'd attended that recent workshop, I was checking out places that offered mediumship messages.

Then my mom and I chatted for a few minutes. I summoned my courage and started, "Um, Mom, I think you know I've been going to this church on Wednesday evenings. Well, they give messages there from people that have crossed over." Silence. I continued on (going further out on a limb), "A medium there brought me a message from your brother Ted. Would you like to hear it? I don't know which parts of it are true."

I waited for a response. Finally Mom said, "Sure, why not?" She was probably intrigued. I had learned to *always* ask permission before giving someone a message; that way the recipient can honestly say yes or no. I'd seen several mediums do that from the stage.

I began relaying the details of the message to her from my scribbled notes, starting with information such as Ted's profession, what he looked like (his distinctive hair color) both of which I knew to be accurate, and then describing a trip he had taken across Europe in a large vehicle. I asked mom if she knew anything about this. "Yes," she said, "Ted did take a trip across Europe in a Volkswagen van after he was in the war. He told me about intense encounters he had as he passed through various countries when officials questioned why he was visiting." Mom went on to explain that Ted was simply curious about the countries, but ran into some "sticky wickets" along the way (I loved it when she used those old expressions).

Gratitude overcame me. Mom was not going to confirm anything in the message if it were not completely true, as she was not emotionally invested in it. I noted the medium that gave this message to me and continued my armchair detective work. Other messages I received were more general, but heartfelt (that can also be quite healing). Still others, from my father in spirit, described accurate nuances of relationships that I could confirm myself. I continued to attend church to see how mediums worked.

During these formative years of my mediumship exploration, I had to discern how I felt about all this. After all, if I was going to be a medium, it might help to actually believe wholeheartedly. No matter. I had to have enough evidence to see how the messages worked before I could truly understand this field. Now I see that messages through mediums help thousands with healing and closure.

Another medium (who has since died) at the church gave messages from spirits to their loved ones in the congregation that were so evidential. You could tell by their responses, and by her conviction, that the information was accurate. After seeing her a few times, I approached Dr. Karen Lundegaard after the service and asked if she taught psychic and mediumship skills classes. Much to my delight, she did, and I signed right up!

After months of attending these services regularly, I concluded that some mediums were bringing through heartfelt and provable messages from specific people on the other side. My father's messages were easier for me to prove, and my mother confirmed several accurate messages from her brother, Ted, and both her parents in spirit.

Chapter 9

Development Circles: A Renowned Master Calling

While I'd taken a few classes and workshops on intuition, psychic development, and mediumship, all on nights and weekends after my marketing position at the financial services firm, it took me a while to find a development circle ("circle"). Surprisingly, it came through a book group I'd found where the focus was books by mediums or on related topics (such as a town full of mediums I hadn't heard of until then, named Lily Dale).

After a few months of attending, I suggested to our wonderful host that those interested in a development circle could meet on another night. He agreed, and we started a small but dedicated circle comprised of a woman who regularly conveyed messages at the local Spiritualist Church, our host, and me. We would meditate and offer messages of a psychic nature about each others' lives, or a mediumship message from one of our loved ones, or friends, in spirit.

Since I was new to being in a circle, I just hoped to learn the ropes and practice receiving and sharing messages from those in spirit. Learning how to deliver a message can be an art in and of itself.

Some circles are "open," with people dropping in on various meeting nights. This circle, we decided, would be "closed" to new members so we could get to know each other, develop safety and trust, and build up the energy. We met on the same day and time each week, and even sat in the same chairs each time.

While we met for a few years in total, this next event surprised me as it happened just after a few months of meeting. I still felt like I was just getting my feet wet with all this. One evening at our regular San Francisco circle, I was drawn to a photo across the room. At first, I brushed it off, thinking I was simply supposed to bring messages out of the ethers from my spot on the couch. I kept being pulled to go to that photo. Finally I explained to my colleagues that I was being pulled to pick up that photo and bring through messages from the man in it (I assumed he was a relative of the host, as there were many such photos in the entry hallway).

I rose from the couch to walk over to the framed picture that was about 15 feet away on the far side of the room. My host jumped up and stopped me with outstretched hand, saying, "Wait! I need to cover up the name on the bottom of that photo." I returned to my seat. The host brought me the photo with the bottom completely blocked with folded over paper. I also put my entire palm over the bottom of the photo so as not to be swayed by any information (about, I thought at the time, uncle Frank or great grandpa Elliot … or whomever this was to our host).

Our host nonchalantly picked up his notebook and pen to write down the messages. The man in the photo told me his family came from fine stock, and named the country he lived in overseas (I'll omit details for privacy); he was honored to have his picture in this room. He found it hard to believe that people still knew who he was … and still listened to his music. He had not been able to do his best work before he died, and that frustrated him. While he had relationships with women, he also had feelings for men. He asked me to convey more on his thoughts about the conditions in which he had to write his music. My brain jumped in for a second. *Hmm, I didn't know our host had a composer in his family.* Concentrating on reestablishing my connection to this man in the photo I heard more, clairaudiently (in my head as opposed to out loud). This is a much different sensation than actively thinking … more about being neutral and receptive. He talked about the love of his life, a man.

He mentioned attributes of his mother and that he loved her very much. The topic changed. While he was here on earth, he said he was not like everyone else, but seen as having special musical talents … but now he noted he was just like everyone else (on the other side). He finished with, "The essence of my soul is loving." Then, humbly, "It is an honor to be here tonight. Thank you."

Our host requested me to ask about his death. I thought, *how difficult it must be for our host if there was confusion around the death of his relative!* So I went back into receptive mode and asked. He conveyed that his death happened in a cold season and went into greater detail surrounding how he passed. But that may reveal his identity, so I'll wrap up here by saying he shared more about his death than was reported. When I finally looked up, our host said to me, "Do you want to know who it is?" I said, "Sure …" thinking that it was probably an elder in his family from generations ago.

He walked over to me and I lifted my palm covering the bottom of the photo, then he took the paper off to reveal the name printed there. I saw the name of a famous composer. I was floored! The entire time I thought this was our host's relative. Why did he have this photo in his living room? He explained that this was his favorite composer and he had listened to his music often. Honestly, I didn't know a thing about him except his name and generally the kind of music he wrote. I shook my head to try to regain my composure after hearing from this composer! We went on with the rest of the circle, but I must confess I was a bit flabbergasted by it all.

Later that night, I took our host's hand-written notes and put them with my other journals in a cupboard … not taking the time to research any of the information that had come through. I was tired and had to work the next day … so drifted off to sleep.

What I Learned

It'd been years since these messages had come through from this composer, and curiosity finally got the better of me. What I learned was that he died at an age where I could see how he felt he may not have done his best work yet. A quick search revealed several articles and sources mentioning his relationships with both women and men, and confirming the country he lived in. I was surprised to learn that this composer was said to have been deeply devoted to his mother. Her death was a devastating blow that he mourned for a long period. Other facts were confirmed that he told me, such as conditions of working for others who he had to write music for.

This story reveals that you never know who you are going to hear from when you open up to do this work. In development circles, I protect myself by opening to only those spirits for the attendees in the room; however, this composer was determined to come through—and there was indeed a connection to our host.

This was the first of a few development circles I have been in over the years. Because they can be hard to find, I sometimes have had to create my own. In this first circle, I persuaded the host to begin the circle in addition to his ongoing book group. I was so thrilled he did and we learned a lot practicing with our third colleague who was more experienced. These development circles were wonderful for me as I could practice and develop my psychic and mediumship skills several times a month. While all mediums use psychic skills like the "clairs" I mention (clairaudience, clairvoyance, etc.), not all psychics are mediums. In circle, we would give each other either psychic messages (about our own life including details on our relationships or work) or mediumship messages (hearing from a loved one, or friend, in spirit).

In my own current circle, that I host and informally lead (as we are all really colleagues), we have slowly added people we thought would be a good fit (as the dynamics of a circle are delicate, and just the right chemistry is needed to foster the supportive, nurturing safety necessary to maximize growth and development).

Back around the time of this first circle I attended, in addition to regular circle practice, I continued to attend psychic or mediumship workshops and classes around my full-time work whenever I could. As the years went by, I began to wonder if I could ever be of better service to more clients one day, or whether this would ever be my life's work. I hoped so, but I set the bar high, making a silent pact with myself that I would need to have a certain level of skill and ability (with provable details coming through) before I would ever make any kind of transition like that in my life. My desire to explore this was about trying to help others.

Chapter 10

Lights, Camera ... and Action

As I was studying the metaphysical world in various ways to try to make sense of my experiences and gain more information, I was reading voraciously on the topics of intuition, psychic abilities, psychic openings (when a person is having these experiences in greater numbers when they hadn't before), mediumship, and channeling.

While reading these books, I learned more about how people who have crossed over can communicate with us in a variety of ways. Something new that struck me as incredulous was the suggestion that spirits can get a sign, or message, to us is through electricity (such as with lamps or even streetlights). At first when I read this, I thought it sounded a little far out.

Since it sounded incredible and I wasn't sure if I believed it, I decided to experiment. Trying something on the sly during my full-time job was also kind of fun. It broke up the monotony of my routine, so I gave it a whirl. So one afternoon while taking a quick break at my job in downtown San Francisco, I decided to try this spirit/electricity thing out. Well, there could not have been a worse place to try this, I thought in retrospect. While in the corporate break room to fill up my water bottle, I noticed the room lighting more closely. During morning and lunchtime, people left the overhead lights on, but in the afternoons—some mood genius on the floor seemed to know how to help us mellow out. The overhead lights were off after the mad rush of the brown-bag lunchtime, so just the pleasant glow of the light under the cupboards was on … casting dim, soft light over the room.

I stood near the door and looked back into the room … thinking, *OK, if this is really true, that spirits can make lights flicker by manipulating electricity, then make those lights over the sink do something unusual.* I concentrated, waiting a few minutes for something to happen (thankful that the room was empty). Nothing. I shrugged my shoulders and went back to work. Granted, I hardly gave it a few seconds, but at least I seemed to have started the ball rolling with my request.

That same week, I was relaxing near the end of the day by reading one of my "woo-woo" books in bed. I fully respect the metaphysical world, but I sometimes poke a little fun at the more airy end of the spectrum by affectionately calling it "woo-woo." I'm a skeptic by nature, so unless something is proven to me absolutely, I don't just jump in and believe it.

As I lay there reading contentedly—with my little grey cat, Scooch, purring deeply beside me—I saw something out of the corner of my eye. I blinked and turn my head to the right. I'd just taken a shower and left the bathroom light and fan on to get rid of some of the steam before I turned all the lights out for sleeping. There was a dim little light on next to my bed, so I could see my book. The rest of my bedroom was dark. That shaft of light from the bathroom spilled out of the door into my dimly lit bedroom, where I was with my fuzzy cat.

As I turned to look I saw the bathroom light (a bulb in kind of a lantern-like holder)—I don't know how else to put it—pulsing back and forth between two light brightnesses. So, one moment, the light was at normal brightness, and a second later, the brightness in that bathroom went up by more than fifty percent to a kind of super-bright glare. Then, the light pulsed back and forth between these two clearly different intensities for several minutes (with the normal light being on for 3-4 seconds, then the super bright light coming on full blast for 3-4 seconds, then going back to the normal light, then repeating … over and over). It was not simply a flickering light, as sometimes happens when a light bulb isn't screwed in all the way. Mind you, this had never, ever happened before in all my nine years of living there. None of the lights in this apartment had ever had any electrical issues, and this wasn't a new light bulb (though it continued to work just perfectly for many months after this).

I lay in bed, I was floored … dumbfounded … flabbergasted. My mouth fell open and my body tensed under the covers then I propped myself up, with my elbows behind me, for a better look. My cat's head jerked straight up from slumber after my movement, then with her yellow eyes open … she also turned to look at the light changing! I thought, this can't be happening. So, I turned my eyes away to the left side of the dark bedroom (toward the direction of the Pacific Ocean, since I was so near the coastline), then back toward the bathroom light. There it was, pulsing so incredibly brightly—it hurt your eyes—then back to its usual every day brightness. It went on and on. Back and forth.

So, ever the skeptic, I jumped out of bed, ruffling the cat that then stood up on the soft comforter. She was still looking into the bathroom at the light show. My left brain was working overtime, trying to make sense of this. I thought to myself again, *If I stand over here by the end of the room, I should be better able to see that shaft of light coming out of the bathroom into my dark bedroom.* I was trying to decrease the variables, so I turned off my dim bedside lamp and stood in my now completely dark bedroom near the north end wall. The shaft of light came out like a rectangle through the door frame into my dark bedroom and I could see this light-changing effect even more dramatically.

Despite my kind of freaking out … the light show went on and on. This was not a light bulb that flickered for a second or was burning out. This was completely unlike anything I'd ever seen or experienced. And, no, I was not on drugs of any kind … not even liquid cold medicine.

So now, convinced of this variation in the light, I thought (my left brain still hadn't given up finding something logical to cling to here), *OK,* **I've** *seen this just after asking for proof that spirits can manipulate electricity.* But there still was that part of me that needed further proof … as I needed someone else to see it! I had a house guest coming to stay with me soon whom I knew quite well. I thought, *if they see this too, somehow, that would really be something!*

I forgot about the incident and didn't mention it to anyone. Why would I? It was so weird! My week continued (with no repeat of this light phenomenon over the next few days or nights). Then, my guest stayed over at my place in my room. The next morning I was getting ready for work and when I checked on them, I learned that the same light phenomenon had occurred. They saw it, too … just as I had. We talked about it that morning and our brains tried to make sense of what had happened. I kind of shook my head in disbelief later that I had asked for a witness … and then that happened.

For the record, never again did any light in the house do this. That light in the bathroom was never faulty in any way, and this never happened again. Why? Probably because I didn't ask. What I asked for first had occurred for me. Then, it happened again when I needed a witness to somehow prove it to me as a kind of confirmation my eyes weren't playing tricks on me. After that, I didn't need to ask anymore. I'd had enough proof that yes, spirits can manipulate electricity. I'd read enough to know that it took an enormous amount of energy (no pun intended) for some spirit to do this, so I wasn't about to waste their precious energy just for my entertainment. What I didn't know was which spirit made this happen. Was it my spirit guide? Was it a relative in spirit? I didn't know at that point. Perhaps if this happened today, I would have the skills to ask the question and receive the answer. Back then, it was just enough to have confirmation that spirits can affect electricity.

I'd noticed that I tended to get answers in paranormal ways when I really seemed to have an emotional need to find the answer. Or, a kind of response came from spirit when I requested something … even if I wasn't fully conscious that I had asked. For example, I could kind of wonder something, without it being a full blown request to spirit per se, and I seemed to get a response (as in this example above). More on that later, but if something was really unimportant, or superficial, I didn't always get answers. When I seemed to have a deeper emotional need, strong desire, or question (either conscious or unconscious), the answer came via an intuition or extrasensory occurrence.

A person who had not had this experience might easily write it off as imaginary. But I have learned that even those who are complete skeptics (myself included, at the start) who have an extrasensory experience, or a visit or message from a spirit who has crossed over, know it was real. But until we have gone through it firsthand, the logical part of our brain kicks in with all the reasons why it is not plausible simply because we don't understand how it happened, or weren't there to know what you saw, felt, or experienced.

However, do you understand how electricity works? How an airplane flies? How your body's healing system works? Is there a scientific way to measure love? I could go on and on with examples of things I may not particularly understand with my logical brain, but they still work (my car engine, etc.). Even if we do not understand how complex things work, they still exist ... and work. It's fascinating that before we have an extrasensory experience, we can doubt another's. Believe me, I value both the left and right hemispheres of our brains for their unique functions, especially since my NDE, which could have permanently damaged my brain.

Remember: we don't necessarily have to understand how something works for it to be real. I certainly was skeptical and tested this out before reaching my conclusions, and I honor whatever belief system my friends, family, and clients have. Understanding comes in its own time, at its own pace. As I've learned over the years of my development, it's helpful to simply stay open.

Action—My Saab Story

After the *lights, camera* portion of this chapter above, this emerged as the *action* part.

Ever since childhood, perhaps because I'm part Swedish, I thought Saab cars were pretty cool. Hey, if you lived in Wisconsin, any car that boasted heated seats attracted your attention! Now, I'll fast forward to my early thirties. I was eating breakfast in my third-floor San Francisco flat on a Saturday morning, admiring the bird's eye view of Golden Gate Park and the tippy-tops of the Golden Gate Bridge peeking through the treetops off in the distance.

As I looked out, an object caught my eye down on the street below. It was a black Saab at the stop sign. As my beloved cat, Scooch, and I watched it drive off, I cleared the dishes and remembered wistfully about wanting one of these cars way back when. I sighed, thinking, *I wonder if I'll ever have a black Saab* … . Mind you, I didn't ever really try to get one (meaning, I never saved for one, or went to shop for one). Frankly, I'm not a big car person, instead preferring to invest in health, connection, relationships, learning, and growth.

So, this moment was more like remembering this desire I had as a young girl, when my mom was car shopping and I tried to sway her to get that black Saab with the heated seats. She ignored my pleas to get the black Saab and bought a sexy blue station wagon. Ironically, she gave me that same station wagon—many years later—during my second year of college. So I ended up steering that tugboat around my college town and was quite happy to have any wheels at all! Still, within my family, it was a bit of a sob story that I never had a chance at getting that Saab.

After that Saturday breakfast, I quickly forgot about the Saab. I went about my business Sunday, and then Monday. On Tuesday, I got an e-mail from a friend that said something pretty close to: *Hey Kay, I know you already have a good car, so I'm not sure why I'm sending this. They are selling this car at my friend's workplace. It used to be the salesperson's car, and now the company does not need it. Again, I'm not sure why I'm sending this, but something made me think of you. By the way, I'm not sending this to anyone else ... just you.*

I opened the attachment just for kicks. Imagine my shock when the photo attachment revealed ... a black Saab! It was the kind I always wanted, with that little pinchy-looking back and the spoiler that looked so cool to my inner nine-year-old self.

Well, this was one of the first instances that made me kind of stop in my tracks and think to myself, *Wait a minute ... I was thinking about wanting a black Saab on Saturday. Now my friend doesn't know why she's sending this e-mail only to me, when I already have a sensible, reliable (read: boring) car.* A part of me could not help but conclude, *Someone out there is actually listening to what I'm thinking and wanting.* My thoughts connected back to classes and workshops where the role of spirit guides was covered. Not having given that much thought prior to this experience, I thought it must be my spirit guides helping with my request. Who else could it be? I didn't know how else to make sense of this. It was so shocking to think that my thought on Saturday was being responded to just three days later!

Even though I could not fully comprehend this quick manifestation of the Law of Attraction—aided by my spirit guides—I knew this was an unusual and uncanny set of circumstances being lined up for me. So, what did I do? I chose to do my part. I rearranged my schedule the next day so that I could drive down the peninsula to the South Bay area. I showed up at that workplace to see and test-drive the black Saab that was for sale. Incredibly, this normally "out of my price range" car was being sold at a price that I could—if I sold my current practical car—afford. Though this made no common sense, I noted these uncanny circumstances and chose to let myself have this car, which was nearly handed to me on a silver platter.

Yes, I had to take steps to sell my perfectly good car. Yes, I had to make that drive up and down the peninsula to make final arrangements to buy the black Saab. Yes, I took all of the tedious logistical steps to make it happen. When the Law of Attraction, aided by your spirit guides, lines something up for you, you can still choose whether to go for what you want or not. I didn't want to live with any thoughts like, "coulda, shoulda, woulda …" So I decided to do the impractical-seeming thing and sell a perfectly good car to get a used car that I had always longed for.

And that Saab was a blast to drive! I don't even care about cars … really. But, every time I turned the ignition and heard that engine start up … Well, if you've ever heard a car start like that, you'd get why this non-car person got excited (and yes, on cold and foggy San Francisco days—which are common—I delighted in hitting that heated seat button).

This powerful example helped me see that my spirit guides exist and are listening to me. They even want me to have what I want! Even though I didn't vocalize to them what I wanted (I just wondered if I'd ever have it … they sent me something more fabulous than *I thought* I could actually have). I saw the signs that they were trying to help, and I followed through. The amazing Law of Attraction can be put into overdrive (or in this case, the turbo kicked in) by sharing your wishes and giving permission to your guides, then doing your part. Either my guides (or my friends' guides, or both) were nudging her to send me that e-mail offering me the photo of the Saab and the opportunity to buy it.

A big part of enjoying this car for the coming years was my allowing the desired car into my life by doing some seemingly impractical things. In your case, the actions may be more practical. Be open to either. If the opportunities show up after you ask for someone or something that seems good for you, will you let yourself have it? Only you can decide what's right for you at the time.

These were initial encounters where I could learn how spirit guides can help us in practical (or emotional) ways. I wasn't completely sure how spirit guides worked yet, but these events really caught my attention. Both the electrical event showing that spirits, or spirit guides, could work with lights, followed by the exact color, make and model of a car I'd always wanted showing up out of the blue had both started with a question that I had thought quietly and hadn't shared with anyone. I noticed that point. The events unfolded after I had asked, simply by thinking about it. Did these events happen because I was being encouraged to learn more, as I seemed to be on a new path after my NDE? Would they occur for another person? I wasn't sure, but I started to piece together what I could from having these initial experiences.

Chapter 11

Premonitions ... "Now We Believe You"

Before I share a premonition I had for a family member while living in San Francisco, I'll backtrack. I had some early experiences in this realm that seemed to be about everyday things. The content seemed unimportant. By premonition, I am talking about knowing about an event before it actually happens, like the experience in Part I where I dreamed about the winning lottery numbers before they were drawn the next day. While that may seem important to some of you, the premonitions that followed seemed very mundane. For example, one was about knowing that a laundry machine I used would be "Out of Order"; the next day, I literally saw that sign on the machine. Not very earth-shattering, right?

Another time, I had a premonition of seeing a quick video-like snippet clairvoyantly. I was sitting in the gym locker room (facing my locker) and someone shoved a combination lock over my shoulder and into my field of vision, asking with an accent, "Do you know how to open these?" Sure enough, the next day I had finished my workout and was putting my shoes on when that exact thing happened. I showed the woman how to use her lock … then I sat there looking at the lockers slightly stunned … recalling the vision from the night before. This premonition may have helped the woman with the accent in some small way, but not in a larger, more significant way.

Perhaps it was from watching movies or television, but I thought that's what premonitions were supposed to do—help people with some important upcoming event. These early premonitions seemed to have simple messages associated with them, like, *Kay, notice this. You have this ability (or better yet, humankind has this ability).*

Apparently, I was hoping that anything that occurred as a result of my near-death experience would be of help to others, but that didn't always seem to be the case (in that larger sense I describe above). When I saw that "Out of Order" sign taped to the washing machine lid, I remembered thinking, *Why would a premonition come about something so everyday like doing laundry?* I made sense of these early premonitions (the laundry and lock) to be to simply let me know I had this ability (perhaps like a preview before the upcoming actual movie).

Fast forward to several years later. I was doing laundry (again) on the first floor of my three-story San Francisco building. After putting the clothes in the (functioning) washer, I was on my way out the door and suddenly was hit with a flash of insight. If you've ever had this kind of experience, you know that is how intuitions can feel—sudden knowledge. I had the sensation that something was about to happen to my brother Carl and that he needed to avoid something to be safe. I shudder to share this part, but I felt that if he didn't, he might be gravely affected.

My left brain jumped in with logic … why am I thinking about Carl? I think he's doing fine. See, even when we are receiving intuitive information, we are trying to make sense of it, sift through it, perhaps even discount it, as I was here. But before my brain could think through this, the clairsentient feelings and clairvoyant pictures surrounding this premonition were about attending Carl's funeral. I was chilled to the core that Tuesday as I walked upstairs and tried to banish this information from my mind.

I thought I'd let go of these unusual "knowings" that Tuesday, but they returned—in full force—the next day. I had a very clear feeling, clairsentiently, that something dreadful was coming up for Carl, but I'd not been given any specifics. Just then, my phone rang. I was happy for the diversion. It was my other brother, Greg, calling to just say hi and catch up. As we were talking, I thought to myself, *I shoved these feelings away yesterday, then they returned strongly today … I think I need to do something about this.* So, as we chatted away, I said, "What's Carl up to these days … is everything ok with him?" Greg replied Carl was fine. I tried to get a clue as to why I might be getting this seemingly foreboding information. Greg said Carl was planning on going sailing with a friend and his own nieces this next weekend on Lake Superior. I quickly jumped in and I knew in that moment the information I received was probably about this sailing trip!

"Oh, no … I don't think he should go," I said. Mind you, I did not say this kind of thing every day. I never had this kind of premonition with a sense of impending danger involved, so I felt a little silly sharing it in case nothing occurred. On the other hand, I felt a tremendous responsibility if something happened and I hadn't shared it. So, I said I was going to call Carl to give him the heads-up about this warning. Greg told me he was just about to call Carl so said he would tell Carl the warning I had received. I urged Greg to tell Carl, "I don't think you should go sailing, but if you insist on going … please wear your life preserver vests." I thanked Greg and we said goodbye.

I thought with a sigh, looking out my kitchen window as Scooch kitty did the same (I'd rigged up a chair just the right height for her so she could comfortably peer out), *I bet people think I'm a little out there when I share these things.* Honestly, it wasn't fun to have this responsibility, to have to sift through what you are thinking versus what might be an intuition, then to share it when people may think you are a little loopy. But I'd rather be wrong and share, and have Carl safe and well, versus not sharing and having him harmed somehow.

Greg called me again on Friday. I eagerly asked him if he'd talked with Carl and given him my message of warning. Greg assured me he had. I breathed a sigh of relief. I thanked Greg and we got off the phone after a little more catching up. After our call, I had a little thought pop into my head, *Great … now I wonder if they both might think I'm off the deep end.* I let this little thought go and sent good thoughts to Carl to be safe.

What is so interesting to me is the irony. What was I doing that Saturday (the same day Carl was going sailing)? I was so excited that I had been invited onto a friend's yacht to sail around San Francisco Bay. Mind you, I'd never done this before! Joining a friend on her boat was most *certainly not* part of my ordinary life of working, classes, and volunteering. It was an unusually sunny, warm day in the Bay Area (where we are often socked in with chilly fog).

So, off I went, and had a fun day in the sun with five friends, catching up, sharing stories and jokes. We took pictures of each other and scampered around the deck for views in all directions. Several times, I hoped Carl would be safe and well on his sailing trip on Lake Superior.

The Calls at Sunset

My day on San Francisco Bay was fun. None of us really wanted the day to end, so we continued chatting on the boat after our captain docked at her usual slip. As we were back near the town of Sausalito now, I thought my phone might work again, so I switched it on. There were several voicemail messages. I moved away from the others so I could hear from a quieter place, looking out onto the bay as I listened to the first message. Once again, it was Greg I'd spoken to earlier in the week, but there was something different in the tone of his voice. As he started to relay an update about Carl, I could tell something was amiss. My body tensed and I attuned my hearing to catch every word. My friends were laughing in the distance.

I was shocked to hear Greg's voicemail message, including that Carl had been out to sail in a seriously bad storm on Lake Superior. Carl was understandably shaken up, but was OK. The storm was so strong that an entire pier with several boats docked there had *broken off* and was now blocking Carl's sailboat's reentrance to the harbor, so they had to tie on to other boats at the next marina down the lake!

The message connected Carl's experience of this intense storm with my earlier warning. Then, Greg said something that rang in my ears for days to come. I didn't expect to hear this, after years of sharing intuitive information with various family members: "Now we believe you."

Next I listened to a voicemail from my third brother, Bill, who also relayed the story of what happened to Carl earlier that day. Bill had also heard about my warning earlier in the week from Greg. Bill's voice mail message was full of surprise at what had happened, and relief that Carl was OK after a very unusual event. I was so glad both Greg and Bill had called me with these updates of the day; I dialed them back right then and there.

Of course, I was just elated that Carl was OK and dumbfounded that he had been in an incident that was dangerous … after receiving that earlier premonition. It was more than odd to rejoin my group of friends who were laughing and talking on our docked boat, when Carl was probably scared witless about not yet being able to get back into his original harbor. I wondered if they were hungry or had water. What a bizarre set of circumstances.

When I reached Carl the next day by phone, I learned more about what had happened to him. He filled in what the previous day was like for him, and explained that he'd also brought his two teenage nieces along for a sailing adventure that I'm sure he thought would be pleasant. The sailboat was 33 feet long; they sailed out onto Lake Superior to simply anchor and spend the night as a kind of adventure. Carl and his sailing friend noticed out on the lake that no other boats were around them. Very odd, on a Saturday, so they listened to the weather updates (there hadn’t been prior weather advisories).

The two experienced sailors learned that a strong wind was screaming up from the south and flying due north toward where they were! What’s more, there were tornado warnings! Tornadoes can flatten many houses as they touch down, so what could they do on a moveable surface, like a huge lake? The two men knew, with the impending bad weather, that they should head back in as quickly as possible. They were about two miles from the marina.

Carl said he had a bad feeling and knew—at the very least—he had to be *so careful.* Carl’s intuition kicked into high gear at that point to help him with whatever might unfold.

Carl said they tried to head in toward the marina. He saw what looked like a black, massive rolling pin up in the sky—a tornado funnel cloud—whirling horizontally right toward them. Carl confided, “Seeing this scared the $*&@! out of me!” He was an experienced sailor, camper, and fisherman. I’d never heard him say anything like this despite having had camping run-ins with enormous, hungry bears (and, ironically, a close encounter with another tornado when he was much younger as part of a boys’ group outing).

As the massive tornado ripped across the sky, with his buddy at the wheel of the boat, Carl scrambled below deck to check the girls. He made sure they had their life vests on and told them to hang onto something tightly, as a storm was approaching. As he did, he glanced at another boat through the window on the left side of their boat. Just then, the tornado screamed overhead. Their sailboat whipped to one side and the window filled with water. He sensed they might capsize. Then the boat flipped violently in the other direction and one of the girls, who was hanging onto her side of the boat, flew across and landed near her sister on the other side of the boat.

Carl tried to orient himself in the chaos. He noticed that the boat he'd seen a few minutes ago was now on the opposite side of their boat! The girls were screaming, and Carl did the best he could to keep them safe. Their 33-foot sailboat was being churned around like a toy in a bathtub. It was tossed ninety degrees several times, as they were slammed sideways onto the surface of the lake in a violent way.

Carl simply said, "I was as scared as you could possibly be. We were lucky …" Also, when they saw no other boats around before the storm and had first listened to the update about the high winds and possible tornado, they headed into the marina for safety because he had recalled my premonition and warning. The girls, his co-captain, and Carl made it out alive. I was so grateful to be talking with him the next day! Hearing these reports of the storm, I was once again happy to be of service for Carl that week as a kind of open telephone line that the premonition could come through.

He added—as we talked about this event when I was writing—that the warning he received from me (via Greg's call) really did help him. Carl explained that he was then on heightened alert … ready to react to whatever peril arose!

Eight years later as I wrote this up, Greg and I were once again chatting by phone. Greg was curious about the date of the storm and recalled Carl telling him the bay of Lake Superior they were at. While we were on the phone, he quickly found the storm date and reports on an Internet search; it was on July 30, 2006. The reports included that a violent storm slammed Bayfield, Wisconsin with few if any early warning signs. Winds were clocked at 90-to-140 miles per hour. I asked for some context to even comprehend winds that high and what they would be like, and he said it would be like a wall hitting you. One person saw a massive tree get ripped out of the ground before his very eyes. After the tornado touched land, there was approximately five minutes of hammering by marble-sized hail. As the tornado winds were able to shift 180 degrees in seconds, it wasn't there one minute and screamed in the next!

While I would not wish a harrowing event upon anyone, I was happy that I could get some information before this event that Carl said helped him know to head back to land as quickly as he could when he heard the weather reports that fateful day. More than that, I'm happy that the potential grave outcome was somehow altered—which to me, is a marvel about premonitions. If we notice them, listen, and have the courage to share them (not easy sometimes, I know), they can sometimes be an opportunity to change outcomes for the better. It's humbling to watch this play out around you.

As I experienced psychic and mediumistic messages coming in for myself and others, it was becoming clearer that this was the direction my life was headed. By this time, I was in my third development circle. This circle had a leader, Felix Lee Lerma, who I'm happy to call a colleague and dear friend to this day. Being in this circle, nearly every Tuesday evening for a few years was just what I needed with helpful information from Felix, and a lot of time practicing to check out how I received messages and fine tune how to deliver them in a caring and compassionate way. I'm so grateful for all the training, practice, and cherished friendships I hold dear from all the circles I've been lucky to find (or create).

Felix had enjoyed a television show featuring a medium that was coming to town to give messages to a large San Francisco audience and he invited me to go. Being game (and curious), I went. I was impressed as I watched her working skillfully one-on-one with some of the approximately 400 audience members. The medium's name was Lisa Williams.

After hearing messages that day given by another wonderful medium, John Holland, the wheels were turning faster. I wondered if I could do this work as I could see how incredibly healing it was for people. While I continued to enjoy my daytime work, I studied and practiced mediumship even more. From the introductory talks each of these excellent mediums gave from the stage, to their evidential and healing messages, along with the classes taken and books I was reading, I learned more about mediumship and spirit guides along the way. I felt it was time to push myself, even if there was discomfort ... it was like a snake shedding its old skin to get to the next supple, fresh layer that would take me even further.

Chapter 12

Spirit Guides, I Have Just One Question

One Tuesday night in my development circle, Felix said he was going to give messages from spirit to a live San Francisco audience one upcoming Saturday and that he had a clear message to invite his circle colleagues to participate. We were really his students, yet there was a nice air of collegiality as he encouraged us to develop. We were honored by Felix's gracious invitation and abuzz about whether we could muster the courage to take him up on it.

The day arrived. I told Felix prior to the message event that I'd meditate from the back of the room (to see if I received some spirit messages) and would give him a high sign if I had connections with spirits to share for attendees. The other circle colleagues decided they would simply watch. They kept poking me in the ribs; was I really going to do this?

As Felix gave evidential and healing messages to randomly selected members of the 80-person audience, I caught his eye and nodded to him. He called me to join him in front of the audience. My legs somehow worked to get me up there. Having watched many others give talks in front of groups, I noted how the speaker's facial expression and body language made it either harder or easier to listen to their talk. It's better to show positivity and momentum, so I put on a smile (despite my inner nervousness) and began to give messages to a few people in the audience from their loved ones in spirit.

The 15 minutes went by in a blur. After the audience's kind applause, I sat in a chair at the back of the room again. Then the most detailed message of the day came to me (after I had just sat down)! A husband and father in spirit directed me to a very sad-looking mother and daughter on the opposite side of the room. He identified many key memories, images, and messages that he wanted me to share with his wife and daughter. After the event, I rushed over to them to ask if they wanted this message (absolutely), and then shared all I could remember and they confirmed all the details he was sharing. They were visibly touched.

Throughout the coming days, I reflected on this message and a few details I had received but had forgotten to include. I wished I could run into the women. In the coming days, I kept thinking back to wishing I could somehow bump into them again (as I had no contact information for either of them). I let that go and went about my work week in downtown San Francisco.

By now, I was living north of the Golden Gate Bridge, and often commuted via transit bus. The trip took nearly 45 minutes, so I had plenty of time to work, or think, or enjoy a little music on my headphones. Since this was a Friday, I was doing more reflecting than working on this bus commute. My thoughts drifted to this ever-growing part of my life—giving people readings and studying mediumship. I had always enjoyed my marketing and education positions in downtown San Francisco, as well as my colleagues. Yet, I wondered which way to go. I thought, *Should I throw myself into my ongoing career? Or would I ever be able to work full-time as a medium?*

I am not one to ask my spirit guides a lot of questions, as I don't want to make them jump through hoops. I'll share more on what I learned about spirit guides over the years in upcoming Chapter 17. I figured, if I ever really needed something important … then I would ask my spirit guides. This was definitely the time to use my "phone a friend" pass.

As I bounced and jostled on the bus along Lombard Street sitting in the very last row, I asked, *Should I just pursue my marketing career, or am I really supposed to be a full-time medium to be of service in helping grieving people someday? Spirit guides, please give me some kind of sign that I will understand so I know where to put my energy.*

I also believed that all answers will come in divine timing—so I didn't want to add time constraints. While I had come to understand that spirit guides are always there for us, I wondered both if I would receive an answer to my question and if I would be able to notice that answer coming to me. As the bus careened down a steep hill toward the Fisherman's Wharf district, I let these concerns go and switched on a favorite song to relax before another hectic day at the office.

I usually grabbed lunch about 12:30 but that Friday I needed to keep pushing on deadlines for my corporate clients. I was beyond hungry and glanced at the clock as I finally left to go get lunch. It was 3:00 p.m. Realizing I was out of cash, I took my automatic teller machine ("ATM") card before heading out to the elevator bank. It felt great to be out in the fresh air for the first time all day as I zipped to the bank across the street to get some money. My ATM card slid into the machine and I quickly punched in my numbers. Silence. I waited and waited, but my ATM card was still inside the machine.

After a couple of minutes, I thought, *Oh, great, the machine ate my card!* I started pushing any button to retrieve my card. Nothing. I knew I could have gone inside the bank to get help, but I thought, *I so do not want to go inside the bank and have to deal with all this. I just want my card back and a sandwich!* I kept punching keys on the machine to try and get my card to spit back out.

Just then, a woman walked up to the ATM machine next to me. Without looking at her, I said, "Oh, hey, just so you know … I hope that machine is working, because this one just ate my card." She looked surprised. "Wait," she said excitedly, "… aren't you that medium who gave me the message from my dad last Saturday?!"

My mouth fell open. This was the very woman (the daughter from the pair I'd spoken with) I had been hoping I would somehow run into, to deliver the final messages from her father that I recalled after we parted. As I tried to collect myself, my ATM card suddenly popped back as I gave her the final messages from her father. She told me how much her mother and she appreciated everything that I brought through from her dad and then remarked how weird it was that we just ran into each other. We then walked in opposite directions on Market Street after our brief exchange.

The San Francisco population in that year, by the way, was 809,249, a number that greatly increases during any weekday because of the thousands of workers who commute in from the North Bay, East Bay, and South Bay, in addition to the throngs of American and international tourists. So, my chances logistically of running into that very woman at the ATM next to me were microscopic.

As I walked away from the ATM, even before I could collect my thoughts about this synchronistic encounter, I ran into an acquaintance that completely supported my mediumship readings and even sent me clients. This was like the second part to this one-two punch of signs that happened within five seconds of each other, messages tailor-made to affirm my direction toward mediumship. There was no longer any need to wonder whether I would *get* these messages!

I began recounting all the factors that had placed me at that ATM at the precise moment to have those two encounters. I never ate lunch so late in the day; I rarely needed to get cash before lunch. The ATM swallowed my card for the *exact number of minutes* until the woman I'd wanted to reach days earlier walked up to the ATM next to me, then the machine spat out my card after I had given her the final messages from her father … well, it was all pretty amazing to reflect upon. Mission accomplished. Signs received. Message answered. Thank you very much!

As is important with spirit guides, I gave them a ton of gratitude for pointing me toward a path I could continue to focus upon. I listened and continued to keep going in that direction while doing the very best I could in my marketing and education work.

PART III

SERVING SPIRIT AND YOU

Chapter 13

Platform Mediumship: Messages from the Stage

Giving one to one messages from a spirit to your client is a completely different setting and experience from giving messages to an audience (large or small). Giving messages to an audience is known as platform mediumship, or a demonstration of mediumship. In this chapter, you may relate to seeing mediums working in front of large audiences on television, in person as a member of the audience, or by watching a YouTube video of your favorite medium(s). Having personally seen some of the best, like world-renowned medium Lisa Williams, these events can be healing, accurate, uplifting, entertaining, touching, and fun. You may see the gamut of emotions, from tears to laughter. It can be fascinating to witness other people getting messages, even if you don't receive one. Sometimes you can relate to a message that is being given to another. Here are a few of my experiences of giving messages in front of live audiences.

Lily Dale, New York: A Whole Town Full of Mediums?

I had a wonderful opportunity to go to Lily Dale, New York, for the first time several years ago. Most mediums know of this amazing, quaint little town, but you may have never heard of it. It's about an hour from Buffalo—where mediums have been giving messages to audiences from their loved ones in spirit for a really long time … .as in, more than 110 years. Think about that for a minute.

I was heading east for a business trip and decided to make a personal side trip to Lily Dale happen, as I'd heard so much about this beautiful town of mediums. I bought a side plane ticket, on my own dime, for a red-eye flight Friday night through Sunday through Buffalo, New York, so I could still be on time for my Monday morning business meetings. I reserved a rental car to drive the hour or so to Lily Dale (from Buffalo), and I dialed my brains out to try to find a hotel to stay in while there (local lodging is often sold out after the Lily Dale summer schedule comes out). Luckily, I found a room in a neighboring town. I've found that much in life doesn't happen unless you *make it* happen (simple, but true), and I am so glad I worked hard to make this personal weekend side trip work.

What was supposed to be my first trip to Lily Dale to just watch other mediums and see what the place was all about, turned out quite different! After the "red-eye" flight from San Francisco to Boston, I hopped my personal "side trip" flight to Buffalo, and then drove to Lily Dale. On about two hours of sleep, I tried to get oriented after parking my car. That Saturday, I took in the readings mediums were giving to large audiences at the lovely, woodsy, Inspiration Stump area.

This is a place where you enter via a lovely trail in a lush wooded area that is designated to remembering beloved pets that have crossed over. As you finish walking this trail, you enter a beautiful area where trees overarch an open area that feels like an outdoor sanctuary. At the opposite end of this area, is the actual "Inspiration Stump" where mediums previously stood atop this large tree stump so their audiences could see them. Now the area is protected by a little fence, so mediums now stand in front of the stump to give messages to the outdoor audiences.

That day, I noticed that readings were being given by Lily Dale registered mediums, visiting mediums from other cities, and—much to my surprise—student mediums. In my slight delirium from little sleep, I thought, *Well ... this is a great opportunity. I should force myself to get up there tomorrow and give messages!* I hadn't planned to, but, I decided to. It seemed easier to watch and take in messages when the mediums delivered them with conviction.

The next day, I signed up to give readings near the entrance to this Inspiration Stump grove. A Lily Dale medium signs you up, noting your name and city on a clipboard for your introduction. What a thrill to be there! The majestic huge trees make a lovely canopy for the benches so people can listen to the spirit messages comfortably. I didn't seem to "get the memo" about the mosquitoes there though, so I was nearly eaten alive over that day and a half as the town is near a large lake where the pesky critters thrive. So if you visit, try to book any hotels or motels early before they sell out (same with appointments for private readings with mediums), and buy repellent in town or you'll end up with the itchy "souvenirs" that I had for weeks.

I meditated before giving messages that Sunday, sitting in this wooded area, which has profound spiritual energy. Visitors often feel an intense feeling of peace or calm. I myself had an unusual experience there. I sat with eyes closed and my palms facing up, resting on my thighs. I was startled to feel something drift down into my open palm, a beautiful leaf, (before the message service began). As it turned out, this leaf was part of a woman's message from her father and it fell into my hand as I was listening to his messages (I made sure she got that leaf later that day).

The place was packed that particular Sunday, roughly 300 people sitting in the grove area to possibly receive a spirit message, as the extremely large crowds had flooded in to take part in a talk that weekend by some ghost hunter television show men. As I meditated before I was introduced, I was drawn to a specific person then given a message for them (and this repeated for about four others in the audience).

Knowing who you are going to give a message to in the audience is a direct message. In contrast, an indirect message is beginning the message with details identifying who is coming through, then asking the audience who can relate to the message (if several people raise their hands, then further identifying who the message is for). In my opinion, there is no preferred way to work … both are great ways to share a message. I've read that mediums debate about which is the better way to work, but as it seems the message is the most important thing, both methods accomplish that.

To be in such a historic setting (you can see the documentary and/or books on Lily Dale) was such a thrill. To connect with audience members there and bring through their loved ones in spirit was an honor (mostly, it happened to be parents in spirit for their adult children in the audience, and a few pets popping in as well).

While at Lily Dale, I attended a helpful workshop by a resident medium. He assisted a gathering of about 40 of us to understand more about connecting with our spirit guides, angels, and spirits on the other side, and explained events that naturally occur with mediums. Even mediums sometimes cannot believe we are really hearing from actual spirits on the other side (as we have that logical part of our brain kicking in as well from time to time). I'll give you an example of this latter point from that first day giving messages in the Inspiration Stump area.

I was introduced to the large audience as a medium from "way out" in California, as many of the visiting mediums were from the East and Midwest. I did not allow myself to think about the size of the crowd due to the normal jitters before public speaking. I prefer to focus on the individuals I have messages for.

I began by raising my voice slightly, as I knew I had to project to the back of that large 300-person crowd. I spoke to a woman in the last row, identifying who I wanted to speak initially with by the color of her shirt and hair. Once we established contact, I said I had her father in spirit who wanted to come through and speak with her. I told her I was hearing the name "Sandy, or Sandra" from him and she quickly said, "That's me!"

As that connection between father and daughter shot through me like an arrow, I thought astounded; *I'm actually hearing from dead people!* As the resident medium shared in his workshop, even though we know from experience that spirit people bring through provable information, a medium's left brain can jump in and almost shout from time to time, *Oh my gosh, I am really hearing from dead people*! ... simply because for so many years as a child and young adult, I thought anything like this was merely the entertaining stuff of movies, and not real (or possible). Well, I used to be a skeptic until I had collected evidence to check out that mediumship was, in fact, possible, with provable evidence that came through (time and time again). The kicker is, a split second after thinking this above ... another part of me thought, *Keep giving messages! You are in front of 300 people!*

The workshop from that wonderful medium in Lily Dale illuminated that this back and forth between our believing then logical sides is not something that can be helped ... it's natural for these different parts of ourselves to chime in from time to time. As a medium, you need to know that is the function of each part of our brain, while the spirit people keep coming through with healing and provable messages.

If you are developing your intuition or mediumship skills, know this is a common occurrence to have both sides of your brain occasionally weigh in on what you are receiving. It's not an issue of confidence, but rather your left brain jumping in with a message that this "does not compute" logically. I actually love it now that both sides of our brain are simply doing their jobs. Both parts are valued, useful, and needed. What does change over time as one gives messages from those in spirit is—there is no doubt that spirit people can come through with both healing, and evidential (or provable) messages. You believe ... no matter that your logical brain still chimes in from time to time.

My time at Lily Dale has left me with so many wonderful memories of watching mediums work and seeing the audience members react to their unique messages. What's more, the setting is lovely and I've never been to another town like it. I was thrilled to have made this personal trip before my week of meetings near Boston.

Backstage Pass: Mediums at Group Reading Events

Many mediums say we are all developing or evolving mediums since we continue to learn and grow and take our skills to the next level. Ever since I really "got" that I was on a new path after several of the psychic and premonition events sunk in, I continued to read mediums' books and take workshops and courses to add to what I'd already learned. The Foreword by Lisa Williams maps out several of the courses I took with her, which were not only informative and pushed you to the next level of development (which I love), but were also a ton of fun. I've met some of the most wonderful colleagues and friends there as well.

Since I love to learn, in mid-year 2012 I signed up for my fourth course (of increasing difficulty over time) with Lisa Williams—a Platform Mediumship course: Taking Communication to the Stage. It was held in October in Southern California; many of the same attendees had taken her Advanced Mediumship Course earlier that year, where we trained, practiced, and were tested.

As I said, there's no comparison between platform mediumship and individual mediumship readings. I had held several small group reading events over the years, but it's a completely different feeling when you are standing on a stage addressing, say, 75 people.

Now imagine not only holding the microphone … but having to tune in to hear what people in spirit are saying and figure out who the message is for in the audience. Keep in mind that most people are terrified of public speaking, where you at least know what you are going to say. Now imagine you are standing on stage, but have no idea what you are going to say, only your faith that you will have a connection to the people in spirit who want to come through, alongside your training and skills.

The reason I share this is … when you see an excellent medium working in front of an audience, they are using so many skills, and my hat is completely off to them! I thought you might enjoy being in a platform medium's shoes. (I don't mean "platform shoes" from the disco days!) I really enjoy watching other mediums do this kind of work. I also enjoy watching television shows about mediums and while they are interesting, in this age of edited programs and videos—group audience message work is LIVE! And that can be especially exciting.

The Platform Mediumship course I attended was a wonderful experience, and I was thrilled to be chosen as one of eight mediums to give messages in front of approximately 75 people from the Los Angeles area. It was a wonderful opportunity to connect some spirit people with their hopeful loved ones in the audience. That day, it was all spirit parents coming through to me, personally, for their adult children and grandchildren there. Despite any normal jitters getting up in front of this crowd (with Lisa Williams watching to boot), I reminded myself it's about trying to be of service for spirit and the audience.

As a little peek behind the curtain, being in the "Green Room" backstage before going onstage to give messages to the live audience was a hoot! There were eight of us back there, plus Lisa Williams was prepping us before we went on. There was so much electricity in that room, I think we could have lit up New York City, and the entire Eastern seaboard to boot! It was a lot of fun, and there was some good-natured joking, as we cracked jokes to let off steam. Some of the mediums were meditating. One was blaring music into her earphones so loudly, we could all enjoy it. I honored that's what she needed to do for her to get ready.

Amidst all this hoopla (and we could not see the audience, so our messages would be truly in-the-moment when we took the stage), we finally got our curtain calls one by one. The first medium was on stage, giving messages to the audience that sounded muffled through the heavy metal door. I was next up, and my heart was racing. Then, I heard the audience applaud and Lisa saying, "I'd like to introduce Kay Fahlstrom!" I burst through the door, smiled and took the mic from Lisa. I was stunned from that moment alone … as I was thinking of her vast experience, working in front of huge audiences all around the world. Then, I had to quickly regroup and start the messages.

It's a wonderful experience to see how you start to receive a message from a person in spirit, and then several people in the audience stand up because they can relate to the information coming through. You have to get specific, evidential information next to help you zero in on which person this message is actually for.

The first message I received was from a father who told me he would be speaking to two people in the audience. Silently I asked for more specific information from this gentleman in spirit … so I'm basically "thinking at" him as I try and collect more information. He answered that he played team sports in high school … specifically, football. When I shared that information, everyone sat down (deciding the message did not fit for their person in spirit) except two people, his adult daughter, and his tiny granddaughter, who could barely see over the chair in front of her. I now had the right people to share this message with. That was a relief as I tried to work quickly so the rest of the audience would not get bored.

Seeing that little granddaughter bounce up and down as her grandfather came through—acknowledging he would never miss a birthday, and her mom saying her little girl's birthday was in a few days—was just so heartwarming. He came through with evidential messages about how he tried to hang on before he crossed over, which was met with his daughter's understandably emotional reaction.

There were many other sweet messages from him for this pair, before I next gave a message for a woman in the front row from her mother in spirit. It was a day of parents for children and grandchildren, and I was thrilled to be part of that backstage group of mediums.

Then we had some unexpected icing on the cake of this memorable day. Lisa Williams herself took the stage and asked the audience if they would like to hear some messages from her. The audience cheered and whooped, "Yes!" So we all enjoyed watching Lisa bring through her incredibly evidential and healing messages—while weaving humor throughout.

During the evening break time in the Platform Mediumship course, I sat in my hotel room for a moment. My mind drifted back to that group message event my development circle colleagues took me to, where I was to see this medium I wasn't yet aware of with hundreds of people in the San Francisco audience that day years ago … I just shook my head in disbelief that I had now taken four courses, of increasing detail and difficulty, from her. I remember sharing this with Lisa Williams later that evening, when we had an evening session of questions and answers. Talking with her about this memory was a little mind boggling as I was truly humbled to have made it somehow from that initial audience to here.

CHAPTER 14

Guess Who's Coming to Dinner?

While nearly all messages I receive are for clients who have scheduled a reading with me, some messages come during the night or very early morning, for those without an appointment. The scheduled readings are requested by the client wanting to hear from spirit loved ones, and the unexpected evening messages are initiated by those in spirit! Feeling so strongly about trying to be of service after I was allowed to come back to earth after my NDE, I'm willing to lose a little sleep if it means someone may be helped by an unexpected message from a spirit loved one.

It's important for mediums to ground and protect themselves regularly (I do this sometimes several times a day). I also decide when I'm open for receiving messages and when I'm not. After I see my clients for the day, I close and re-protect myself (so spirits cannot pop in all evening or during the night). Despite my not being "open for business" during my sleeping time, some spirits are pretty determined to get through and sometimes they do. When they get my attention, and I can feel clairsentiently who the message is for, then I always try to pass it along after I ask if the recipient wants to hear it. On another note, I have also noticed that when I'm on a week of vacation from working, I'm much more relaxed and these unexpected spirit messages can sometimes flourish.

When this event occurred, I was still working a full-time job in downtown San Francisco. Like many other mediums that develop over the years, we give readings and sit in development circles around our daytime work. Luckily, I really enjoyed my jobs over the years, and thoroughly enjoyed giving readings for visitors in development circles as well. So, I was taking a week off of work on a "stay-cation." I'd planned to simply relax at home and watch movies, catch up on things, and had weekend plans to see friends. That Tuesday evening, I was at the movie rental store looking for some movies that suited the vacation mood, but was drawn to renting "The Reader." Later, I relaxed and watched this movie. It was rather late that night by the time my head hit the pillow.

Very early the next morning, I was awakened and could tell I was getting a rapid download of messages from a man in spirit. Luckily, I had a pen and a pad of paper close to the bed. I glanced at the clock. It was a few minutes before 5:00 a.m. I took several pages of notes from this man in spirit. I could feel who this message was for (a prior colleague, Pete, for whom I still had contact information). The man identified himself as Pete's father who'd suffered an unusual death. His son had found his dead father, sadly from a suicide.

I thought to myself, *Pete doesn't even know I am a medium, and I have to call him and see (delicately) if he wants to receive this message from his dad, after I explain I can hear from people who have died.* These moments are when I know I did not choose this gift, it chose me. Don't get me wrong. I cherish and appreciate this ability I was given during my time on the other side, as it helps people feel more comfort, closure, and healing. However, at moments like these, I sometimes think to myself, *Here we go … let's hope this goes well.* You certainly get all kinds of reactions from people when you are simply trying to honor the wishes of their loved one who has passed away.

I hadn't talked with Pete in quite some time and it had been many years since I had actually seen him. I dialed his number, holding my breath a bit, and left a voicemail; thinking quickly how to summarize this side of me he didn't know about and also that I had a message for him from his father who had died.

Trying to leave an out for Pete, I said to call me back if he wanted to. When I receive unexpected messages from a spirit, I feel an obligation to try my best to pass along the message. Yet, I always ask people who are not expecting a message if they want to hear it and respect whatever answer they give me. If they say "No, thank you," I simply talk about the San Francisco 49ers or the Giants and catch up with them about their life. If they say "Yes," I pass along the message, being careful to explain a little more about spirit communication if they have never had a reading before.

Only a few hours went by before Pete called me back. He said he didn't know I was doing mediumship, but he was very interested in hearing the message from this father. He asked for a call back and left his work and home phone numbers. I called back that Friday late in the day and missed him, so left another voicemail asking for some times he'd be around when we could talk. Thinking I probably wouldn't hear back from him over the weekend, I simply let the whole thing go (and knew we'd probably catch up the next week).

The next evening, my friend and I were enjoying a leisurely dinner together at my home. I started to notice a feeling behind me and brushed it off, but the feeling returned. My back was to my little galley kitchen as we sat at the oak dining room table talking and laughing. Now it became clearer that we were being watched by this presence. This isn't a sensation I'd had in my home before, as I'm very careful to only open myself for the one client I am giving a reading to (that is, I am only allowing spirits connected to my client to come through to me). Since I always "close down" after a reading, it was a first that I felt a spirit hanging around after my work week.

There was irritation or impatience coming from this presence. I could feel their eyes boring into the back of me, but when I turned to check if I could see them, I could not see the spirit with my naked eye. Yet, the presence was entirely palpable. I really did not want to make my dinner guest uncomfortable, so I quietly endured. Finally I said once, "I feel like there is someone watching us … right behind me," and I motioned to the kitchen hallway. Then, I continued to talk away, not wanting to alarm my friend any further. I didn't realize I'd have a second dinner guest!

Later, I was standing at the sink rinsing dishes when I felt the presence of the spirit move behind me, which was quite unexpected. I had sensations in my body as the spirit literally brushed against my back as it moved toward the dining room table. I felt a cold and clammy feeling crawl all over my skin. I was shocked at this.

I had been giving thousands of readings to people, both in my professional office (and in my home office) for some time and I had never experienced anything of this sort in my home. I stood there silently, and then grabbed a light jacket to put on in an effort to warm up my back as it still had that unmistakable chill on it.

Just then, I flashed upon another experience that was similar to this. As I tried to continue to talk nonchalantly with my dinner guest, I thought about my first visit to the infamous Winchester Mystery House in San Jose, California. Sarah Winchester continued to build and build this house, without ceasing, until she died (you can learn more about this story there or online). When I was touring the Winchester Mystery House, I wanted to see if I felt anything there as a medium, as I'd read a book by a psychic who was called in to try and cross over the ghosts that were reportedly there. Alas, I was disappointed because I felt nothing unusual on the first two levels of the house. I am by nature quite skeptical, and need to make sure I collect my own information and felt body sensations first before I'll even entertain believing in something.

As we finished the house tour, we went on one of the top levels of the house, through the hallways and rooms of the servants' quarters before returning to the main floor. As we walked through the hallway closest to the servants' quarters, I still felt nothing. We were allowed to go into the room where some of the servants had slept. I went in nearly last … letting the rest of the tour people move along so I could have some time in there alone. The air in that servant's room felt heavy. I had a cold, clammy feeling of dread. I could feel a ghost, or more than one, in that very room with me. I could feel they were to the right of me and behind me … near where the bed in the room was located.

A sensitive person can feel these subtle differences in energy and where the entity is in the room. The spirit energy in my home that Saturday night with my dinner guest felt the same way. I then knew I didn't have a fully crossed over spirit person in my home that evening. I had a person who was stuck between our earth world and where the vast majority of the spirit people I normally hear from are—the other side. Some mediums call a person who—for whatever reason—does not want to fully cross over to the other side … a spirit trapped in the vortex. Most of us have heard this kind of spirit, or entity, called a ghost.

Back to my trying to entertain on a Saturday evening in my home. I went into the living room to build a fire in the fireplace. After I got the fire lit, I sat on the hearth, with my friend opposite me in an armchair I'd pulled up near the fire. I started to feel the presence of that same spirit again. He had moved from the kitchen to just behind me on the left … he was in an alcove kind of space in the corner (and this vertical shaft of space shot up to the highest point on the vaulted A-frame ceiling). So, this spirit was hovering about four feet to the left of me and about four to five feet above where I was sitting. Again, I decided to say nothing (not wanting to alarm my guest).

But—feeling more unsettled as the night went on—I decided to set a boundary with this spirit before going to bed. As I noted this presence was not leaving, I was mentally sending updates asking this spirit to find other lodging for the night. This did not seem to work, so I felt pretty strongly about drawing a line in the sand. As communications with spirits are telepathic (that is, thought to thought), I said to him, *If you insist on staying all night here, you are to stay in the living room! You are NOT welcome in my bedroom!* Thankfully, this presence respected my wishes. I had no sensations of this spirit watching me as I slept.

I was so relieved when Pete called me late the next morning to say he'd love to hear the messages from his father. I reviewed the notes I had scribbled at 5:00 a.m. five days earlier and called him back. When he answered, I gave him an overview of how mediumship messages come through, as he'd not had a reading with a medium before.

Pete listened to each message. I told him that I was awakened early in the morning just after watching "The Reader." The movie chronicles one woman's experience of life during World War II and the Nazi Germany regime. Pete said his family and the man who came through to me were Jewish, and that the family had decided to escape the atrocities occurring at this time. The plot of this spirit visitation was starting to thicken. It was already unusual for me to get a full-blown message reading without a scheduled client … and the subject matter of that movie was not what I would typically choose for my normally lighter fare during a week of vacation. There are no coincidences … only synchronicities, as I came to learn after my NDE.

I was being very delicate in passing along these messages to Pete, as I could empathize that this was an unusual experience for him. It seemed quite important to me that I go slowly and deliver the messages with much care. Pete could validate that this was his father by confirming the way he crossed over, along with many other messages that came through to me, including his dad giving a street name from the town they lived in (with which I was not familiar … but confirmed a few days after this phone call with Pete).

Pete was very gracious during this call, and once muttered, "This is fascinating." After I gave all the messages, he said that his relatives had told him much about his father during the last few months. So, while my call came out of the blue, he could also put it into context. The mediumship messages dovetailed nicely into this river of information.

Pete confirmed facts and first names of people mentioned in this unexpected reading. However, there was a key point to this message: more than anything else, his father wanted to be forgiven (for committing suicide, and for arranging it so that Pete would find his body, instead of his wife).

"Yes, I have forgiven him," Pete said. But I had to reiterate, "No … you *really* have to *mean* it!" It is not like me to be so emphatic, but there was a reason this spirit had me choose a certain movie as the backdrop to this reading, then woke me up at 5:00 a.m. with his plea. I have heard from enough fully crossed-over spirits to know that Pete's father was *not* fully crossed over and on the other side.

I told Pete it would be great if he could take time after our call to once again, with pure intention, forgive his father, who seemed to really need his son's forgiveness in order to move on fully to the other side. Pete's father was a ghost, in-between the earth and the other side … who desperately wanted to be forgiven for his act of suicide, which was undoubtedly etched in Pete's memory, and which his father now regretted.

So why did his father come to *me*? Because I knew Pete and how to get in touch with him. And, I happened to be a medium.

After this action-packed vacation week and weekend, I also put the last part of it all together. Pete's father was hanging around my home Saturday night almost as if to say, "Pass along the message to my son … now, please!" He had already waited four days! Thank goodness Pete called me back Sunday. I was truly grateful I was able to help both Pete and his father. It was a profound experience. I had helped ghosts cross over, but never from the comfort of my own home!

Chapter 15

A Story of Crossing Over

While there were many years of me giving messages to my family, and many years of me flying back to visit family, the visits increased when I knew that I'd have only so many years left to see my mom. From my early twenties, after I moved from Michigan to California—and for most years thereafter, I'd seen my mom and family once or twice a year. I'd make the trek from San Francisco through Minneapolis or Chicago on to Wisconsin for a visit. The frequency of these visits changed after 2002 or so, as I felt I should go back as often as I could because of my mom. In the final few years of her life, I was visiting more like three or four times a year, and sometimes even five or six times.

I'm so glad I did visit more often during those years, as I knew that people, and things, don't last forever. Not to be too blunt, but I knew first-hand from my near-death experience that there was (at least for me) nothing very ceremonious about dying. There is no disrespect in that statement. Before I nearly died … then was allowed to come back, I thought that one's death would be monumentous or ceremonious (with some kind of foreshadowing or prelude leading up to it). But, for me … after my NDE, I knew it was neither. All I mean is … one day you can think you have the flu bug, then you go to sleep that night … and then you die. It can be that simple. I was alone. I felt sick. And, I died. No fluff. No stirring music from off-screen. No company (except my cat). So the silver lining in having this experience … and there are actually a lot of silver linings—is the unique perspective it brings to live your life each day, to tell people who are important to you how you feel about them, to allow yourself the positive feelings about yourself (instead of just focusing on the negative), to let yourself have some simple (or more grand) pleasures along the way, and to be who you really are.

One of the things I really *know* after my NDE is to cherish every day, try to do the best I can, and enjoy the moments along the way be it a sunset, laugh with a friend, yummy meal, or phone call with someone you care about. As a simple reminder, I once wrote a sticky note that just said, "SAVOR EVERY SECOND". These things may sound cliché, and I can appreciate that if a person has not had a near-death experience, it might be difficult to really *get* that our lives can end at any moment. I say that with understanding and compassion.

Here is a much different kind of passing, my mother's, one that was more expected than a person in their early twenties, although none of us are really ready to say goodbye to a loved one … let alone, our own mother.

Prelude

I remember getting a call early one morning while on a business trip in Phoenix, Arizona. I can visualize exactly where I was standing in my hotel room, by the mirror in the white marble bathroom, absentmindedly brushing my hair, listening to my cell phone calls shortly after waking up. I heard my sister on voicemail, telling me that our mom had to be rushed to the hospital in the middle of the night by an emergency squad. I dialed my sister back immediately. She was amazing, talking about what happened in as calm and even manner as possible, perhaps not to freak me out.

Her years in the medical profession were evident in how skillfully she shared this news with me. I asked questions about how mom was, and asked if I should I fly back to see her now. My sister tried to reassure me. I remember asking her, "I wonder if this is the beginning of the end?" Our mother was 82 and all of her siblings and parents lived about ten fewer years than that. Mom was suffering from a health condition and was now in the hospital, receiving care. I couldn't help shake the feeling that this might be the beginning of the end … as much as I did not want that to be true!

That last day of March, 2008, I was in a daze as I packed up my business meeting presentations and clothes and headed for the Phoenix airport to fly to California. Afterward, I was back at work in San Francisco for a week or so, and I remember getting a call at my work desk, hearing my brother talk about how much care mom needed at home since her emergency hospital stay. I'd never done anything like this in my entire career, but I started to fill out the paperwork for a Family Leave, and spoke with my supervisor about my mother's condition and my hope that I could go help her when she really needed it.

Everyone was wonderful at work and I flew back to take care of mom, alongside some of my siblings who lived close by and had been helping ongoing. Mom needed around-the-clock care now. This time I spent with my mom was precious, helping take care of her and sleeping when I could, as several of my siblings had done for some time. But after being there several weeks, I needed to return to work. My mom and siblings and I talked about this plan, which seemed like a good one, as we'd hired a night aide so my siblings could help more during the day.

I remember the morning I had to fly out to return to San Francisco—Cinco de Mayo. I'd zipped out early to get some Mother's Day gifts for her, so they would be there for her the following Sunday. Before running off to the airport, I wanted to be with mom in the makeshift bedroom created for her on the first floor of our house. So, instead of eating a quick bite at the kitchen table (two rooms away), I asked her if I could perch on her bed instead. She agreed, and I told her little stories of things I'd seen that morning as she was cooped up in the house, unable to walk enough to see outside the windows.

As I talked about the little girl I'd seen that morning on our block, zooming around on her little bike with her pink streamers flying in the breeze from her handlebars, my mom smiled broadly, imagining that simple sight. She was enjoying hearing the stories of everyday little things that I shared from what I saw outside that morning. I felt very uneasy, knowing I'd have to say goodbye and leave soon. For years, with me flying back to San Francisco from Wisconsin, you couldn't help but wonder if this would be the last time you might see her. My stomach was nearly churning this time, as she'd been so ill since Christmas.

I got my luggage together by the front door, put my coat on and now sat by the side of her bed. This was very uncharacteristic of our goodbyes, which were usually a hug … but I hugged her, then kissed her cheek and I recall saying, "Take good care" in a soft voice. I couldn't bear it, but I had to make myself turn and go out that door to the airport.

(As I prepare this book manuscript to release it to the printer today, it is Cinco de Mayo once again … six years after this May 5th day I'm describing above. I did not time this … and could not help but share this detail with you.)

After a day of travel that felt like a haze, I tried to settle back into my work and life. I also tried to be grateful for the extra time I'd had with mom, despite how she was struggling. About two weeks later, my sister got a brand-new puppy and drove up to visit mom on her weekend off to show her this cute, fuzzy ball of golden fur. They had a nice visit and my sister had to go back home for work. The next day, I started to get calls from siblings with the update that mom had now really taken a turn for the worse. The hospice workers that periodically came to check on her said she was "actively dying." I was at work on that Monday, and I had a client to see that evening between 6:00 and 7:00 p.m. It goes without saying that was a really hard day to get through.

That evening at 5:55 p.m., I don't know what possessed me to listen to a cell phone message right before going in to sit with my client for an hour, but I did. My brother told me that mom had just crossed over. I was stunned. The enormity of this moment cannot be described. *How in the heck*, I wondered, *was I going to listen to my client for an hour now?* Why, oh why, did I just listen to that phone call? I walked up the block to the office, telling myself that I needed to keep it together for one hour, as my client deserved my full attention.

After I somehow got through that hour, I called my siblings immediately. Many of them were there in the house we all grew up in, with a few others still in their home states. My oldest brother relayed to me the final moments with mom. I share this with you as one experience of what it's like to leave the body.

Gentle Transition

My brother started to tell how mom asked him to sit with her in the early evening on her bed. She'd been really groggy for the last day or so. She asked my brother to hold her, which was very uncharacteristic for her and said she was scared. My brother is a big, strong man and he put his arms around our mom and hugged her. She said, "Hold me." He replied, "I am, I'm really squeezing you." Mom said to him, "Hmm … I can't feel it." Perhaps a part of her consciousness had already left her physical body.

After a few moments, she called to someone in the distance, "John!" She was seeing someone she recognized. There are two other relatives we have named John (and they were both still alive), so my eldest brother, who was holding mom, said truthfully, "Yes, John will be here this weekend." I think mom was seeing a different person named John that she knew maybe from much earlier in her life … I don't know.

Next, mom said, "It's OK … you don't have to hold me so tightly … I'm OK now." Then, after a few moments, she ventured, "I think I might jump in …" She was considering it. At this, my brother shared with me later that he thought then, *You mean, the 'little jump in' or the 'BIG jump in'?*

Again, after a few moments, mom finally said, "I'm going to float away now …" and my brother tearfully related to me on the phone that he said reassuringly to her, "It's OK, I'll float along beside you if you like …" Then, he laid my mother down, and went into the kitchen area to tell my sister what had just happened. My sister had just raced back from her home two hours away to be there.

When my siblings went back in to check on mom, she had already crossed over.

I'm hopeful that sharing this account of crossing over helps you see that it can be gentle, and that fear can lessen as the crossing over starts to takes place. What's more, it can include reunions with people we've known that are pleasurable. It's also remarkable that mom seemed to have a choice about when she decided she wanted to jump in and float away.

Chapter 16

How Spirit Loved Ones Can Get Your Attention

We can hear direct messages from our loved ones on the other side through a medium, or even receive a message ourselves (whether we are awake or asleep). It's remarkable that as technology advances, people in spirit are using cell phones, digital pictures, and computers to get messages across to us … along with a variety of other ways to get our attention.

Aside from the newer methods of communication noted above, people in spirit have used animals, songs, electricity, coins, compact discs, land line phones, and more to get a message or sign across. After reading some of the examples below, you may recognize your own spirit messages from loved ones more easily.

Messages Through a Medium

One of the most common ways people receive messages from their loved ones in spirit is by visiting a reputable, ethical, well-trained medium. Some mediums offer 30- or 60-minute reading sessions where you receive messages from your loved ones in spirit that have passed (or crossed over). I hear trepidation from just a few potential clients who think this is possibly a spooky experience. Quite the opposite. In fact, I delighted when a recent client said just that …"This wasn't spooky or creepy at all … but it was really great to hear from my family!" Seeing a legitimate medium is positive and helpful, and is like any other completely professional experience. When you go to visit a doctor, she or he is clearly well-trained and the office environment is well-lit, welcoming and comfortable. Same with a financial advisor, medium, or any other professional who is well-trained in their field.

Do Mediums Get Messages for Themselves?

My clients often ask me if I am able to receive messages for myself from my loved ones in spirit. The answer is yes and I've included some of those examples below. An after-death communication (ADC) can come in many forms, as varied as each of our senses. A common way is smelling something connected to your loved one in spirit as they may be simply trying to say "Hey, I'm OK! It's me and you'll know it by the smell of my perfume." Or, a spirit can make you smell their cigarettes, or something more pleasant like the blueberry muffins they loved. One can also see, taste, or hear something that makes them know it's their loved one trying to come through. Below is one such example.

Hearing Out Loud

I received two clairaudient (that is, I could hear them with "clear hearing") messages from the same spirit at the crack of dawn. These were heard in my head. It took me hours to "get them" though. First I heard some noises that awakened me abruptly: the sound of a loud crash of pots and pans, then of an exasperated person saying "S**t!" I wondered what kind of spirit person was trying to come through to me with this odd combination of sounds, but I rolled over and went back to sleep. I had to commute to, then work all day in, San Francisco and later bus back home (about 11 hours total).

Next I heard, clear as a bell near the right side of my head, my mother's voice say one of my childhood nicknames as no one else pronounced it. "KAY-ba!" Everyone else in my family said it with even emphasis on both syllables (and more slowly than she did). The fact that I heard this out loud, in my bedroom, was shocking! Hearing something out loud from a person in spirit has only ever happened to me this one time.

After hearing this, I wanted to try to connect to my mother, so I reached my right hand from under the covers to her. I knew I could not feel her hand if she grasped mine, as she now had an energetic body, or light body, but I wanted her to know that I knew she was visiting me. Well, she certainly did get my attention! I was very touched she had spent all that energy to materialize her actual voice. I had to chuckle. I knew she was the spirit behind waking me up with the pots and pans crashing (and the expletive). I called my sister and nephew back in the Midwest to share these messages by phone later that morning, as I could not place why she was making me hear crashing pots and pans.

About noontime, when I was taking a quick coffee break from work, I checked my cell phone voicemail messages. My sister said she had some answers about the pots and pans. I called her back. She said our eldest sister, who is a marvelous cook, was cooking up a storm that day but things just were not turning out right for some reason. That frustration could explain the expletive. It was like mom was sharing a little inside joke that she knew what was going to happen, and we all had a good laugh. Pretty funny, as that kind of language was not mom's style, but she certainly still had a sense of humor!

Dream Visitations

In Chapter 2, I describe being visited in a dream by my father who had been in spirit for 13 years. It was a wonderful message, and also kind of a foreshadowing of the mediumship messages I started to receive myself, described in Part II of this book. I've also had a few dream visitations from my mom after she crossed over in May of 2008.

Here are main characteristics, some outstanding hallmarks of dream visitations: the colors can be unusually vivid, a kind of light can emanate from the face or body of your loved one in spirit, they may look much younger than when you last knew them, you will "get" what your loved one is trying to say to you, even though it may be telepathic (that is, thought to thought, without verbal words being exchanged … so their mouth may not move to form the words but you will still get the message), and when you awaken, you will feel that it was a real interaction with your loved one.

These dream visitations can be very brief. Finally, you may even think, "But … dad, this can't be you … you are dead."

Or, "Oh good! We dodged the bullet of his illness … he is OK and with me now so he is healthy after all!" I include because these dreams feel so real (because they are), you can think the person is alive again. So, while it's wonderful to see and interact with your loved one again, there can be that moment of realizing they are still in spirit. Even still, my clients report loving these dream visits!

Also, your person in spirit can be wearing different kinds of clothing than they did here. My mother shows herself in clothing she did not actually own, that I have never seen before. So just be open to the fact that they can show themselves as young and healthy and good-looking (with a full head of hair, or a small waistline … even if it's not how you remember them at the end of their life).

Other Signs

Some examples of ways people in spirit try to get our attention could be called a coincidence. But I've known people who were touched and knew it was their person in spirit getting their attention, because of the content or timing of the message, or as a response to their telepathic question. These are perfect examples of meaningful coincidences. But when these communications are meaningful to the receiver of the message, they are no longer coincidences—but rather, synchronicities. Listen to the heartfelt conviction in someone's voice after they have received a message to know a real connection was made with their person in spirit.

Here are some of the ways people in spirit can try to get a sign to us.

FAUNA (ANIMALS)—I have heard and read about countless experiences people have had with some kind of animal (or even insect) where they felt it was clearly a sign from their loved one in spirit. Hummingbirds and butterflies are examples I hear about often. One example of such a message was from a woman while on a long-awaited vacation to Hawaii. Here's what happened:

"After traveling all day, I laid down for a little nap. Suddenly I was awakened by a bird that was very close to the sliding glass door on the lanai (outdoor deck). He perched on the back of a lawn chair (only about 2 inches from the glass door) until I sat up and looked at him. This bird stayed and stayed, looking right at me, squawking loudly. It felt like a welcoming committee from my mom who had passed away years ago … as I bet she was thrilled I was on her favorite island. The squawking continued for more than 6-7 minutes, and then never happened again during that entire time away."

As I said, many people relate stories about how seeing a butterfly gave them a sign from their loved one in spirit. Or, the sign can come from other small animals (birds, ladybugs or other insects, chipmunks, squirrels, fish) or larger animals as well.

Having heard two stories first-hand about people seeing owls soon after their loved one crossed over is interesting, as Native American symbolism of the owl includes an association with death and spirits. The owls can be seen, by some tribes, as a spirit of the person who passed or as a powerful spirit protector (alltotems.com).

I, myself, had a message for a person I knew from a sibling in spirit that included an owl reference. The person the message was for could not place the owl reference. Later that very warm night (after I gave the rest of the messages), my windows were wide open to try and cool my bedroom down. I changed my sheets as I got ready for sleep. As I did this routine task automatically, I started to hear a sound. I stopped to focus on the sound. It was an owl sounding, "Whoo whoo!" over and over again … from a pine tree branch about 10 feet from my open windows! I just stopped and listened … kind of astounded as I had never, ever heard an owl while living in this same home for more than five years.

The owl hooted on for about 20 to 25 minutes—and I listened … transfixed. Then, the owl flew the coop. I have never since heard an owl near my home and it's been about 18 months since this happened. The same day the message was passed along to its recipient, the owl confirmation came. Just to give a ballpark estimate, I did not hear an owl on more than 2,300 days or nights of living in this home … so hearing one that night certainly completed the reading as the owl reference then made perfect sense. One could see it as a kind of thank you for passing along the messages.

FLORA (PLANTS)—People share stories of seeing a certain plant or flower and know this is a message from a person in spirit. For example, one might see a plant or flower blooming in the winter, and they know this is a message from their loved one in spirit who loved that particular kind of plant. Once, while I was giving a phone message, the man in spirit talked about the woman I was speaking to receiving flowers. Much to both our amazement, the doorbell rang and friends spontaneously gave her a bunch of flowers at that moment!

RAINBOWS—A client sent me a photo of her seeing a rainbow after she arrived on a Hawaiian island and knew it was clearly a message from her loved one in spirit welcoming her there. Others see a rainbow as a good omen, or an affirmative answer to a question they put out.

COINS—While I haven't experienced this myself (yet), I've heard reputable mediums talk about spirit people leaving a coin where you can notice it. Some check the year on the coin to see if it is meaningfully related to the person in spirit (i.e. birth year or anniversary of a passing, or other important year such as a marriage or graduation). I have a close relative who reports receiving coins from her spouse in spirit … the coins are always heads up. Heads or tails, finding a coin can feel meaningful to the person finding it.

I personally would not find seeing a coin *outside* as a sign, but one indoors would catch my attention. To better test this method of receiving a sign, I keep all coins in a jar in the cupboard so if I come upon a coin elsewhere in the house, I'll notice it.

Below is another example of a spirit communication. Some of these spirit communications may not translate well to a reader who has not yet had this kind of communication themselves. But, rest assured, when people do, they call me and tell me directly, saying, "I cannot tell anyone this experience but you. Others would not believe me." They seem to need to share the experience to anchor it, and feel they are not imagining it. Wherever possible, I try to listen and ground these experiences for my clients and students, as I recall those who helped me with mine.

MUSIC—Spirit people can get us a song with lyrics that are just perfect when we flip on the radio, or shuffle our songs on a device. Here's an example of a musical message from that long-awaited few days off to Hawaii I mentioned earlier (the message wasn't even clear to me until just an hour before I flew back home). As I note in Chapter 15, when mom was quite ill (a few weeks before she crossed over), she had trouble breathing despite being on supplemental oxygen. Often, she'd awaken in the middle of the night, and I'd jump up to see what she might want to help her relax and fall back asleep. One of her favorite things was a Hawaiian music compact disc (CD) of a singer nicknamed "IZ." He sang a beautiful rendition of "Somewhere over the Rainbow." As she listened to this CD, mom could often finally relax and get a tiny bit of sleep—perhaps as it may have harkened back to her beloved trip to Maui.

While I did know that this island was one of my mom's favorite places on earth, what I did not know was that same IZ CD was in my rental car the whole time I was there. The craziest part of all this was, I never used the CD function during that week … so I never heard the IZ CD in the car! I'm sure I would have burst into tears if I had (and known mom made this happen, as it inextricably bound us together).

On the final day of my vacation, I returned the rental car and got on the airport shuttle. The car rental guy ran after me as I sat on the car rental shuttle, and he suddenly shoved a CD into my view as he said, "Ma'am, is this your CD? You left it in your car." It was a CD of "IZ." It all happened so fast, I could not even compute it, as the shuttle driver wanted to get going. I was confused. I thought, *This is not my CD.* I had to be honest and say it wasn't mine and he left with it. Then it hit me as we drove off toward the terminal. It felt clear to me I received the message about the connection to mom, that beloved lullaby, our time hearing it together, and my current location she loved dearly. That IZ "… Rainbow" cover song still makes me cry instantly, even today.

NUMBERS—My students who study intuition, psychic, and mediumship abilities in my classes often report seeing a certain number on the clock repeatedly (such as their birth month and date). This is much easier to note on digital clocks than face clocks, it seems. For example, I marvel at the many times during a day when I glance up at the clock and see the hour ending in "11," as, 3:11. You may have a different "hit" about what your number means to you; perhaps nudges from a loved one in spirit, or from a spirit guide (more on that topic in the next chapter). The meaning of seeing the particular number is unique for each person.

TELEPHONES—Spirit people have been using telephones to literally dial their loved ones for decades; the person on the other end may hear anything from silence to static to a voice (even if it's faint), or a message (though this is extremely rare).

CELL PHONES—This type of telephone after-death communication has evolved as technology has. I have two clients who reported to me that although the cell phone account of their deceased loved one had long since been cancelled, they each received a call. As the phone rang, to their astonishment, the name of their dear person who had crossed over showed up on the screen! I cannot explain how this happens, but people in spirit can manipulate electricity and phones.

COMPUTERS—Here's an example of a person in spirit using a computer to get a message through. The person reporting this to me was at work when this happened. When this clairsentient professional learned of her client's crossing over, she not only had a personal experience of sensing this same spirit coming to say hello a few days later, but there was also a second message. The professional started up her computer to begin the day's work. A message showed that the person who had crossed over had been "Discharged" from the database of records (and also listed her name). However, her file was still completely active and *had*

> *not yet been* changed to the "Discharged" status … so there was no logical way that initial notice could have shown up on her computer.

How much energy does it takes for people in spirit to create these kinds of messages for us? Can they only send so many messages every year? Can they only come through in a vivid dream visitation once in a blue moon? Some people only ever have one cherished visit from their loved one in spirit. It takes work for them to bridge the difference in energy vibration between our denser, more slow-moving world and their other-side world of higher, faster, more subtle vibration. I try not to expect the messages at all, so that when they do occur, it's like a wonderful gift out of the blue.

You can experiment with asking for a sign that you will understand from your loved one in spirit. Then, be open to whatever kind of sign he or she can get through to you (versus being attached to a message coming in a specific way, say … via a yellow butterfly only, or something else). It may come in a way that you don't expect … which can be part of the mystery and fun.

Many things are possible in the spirit world. Be open to however a message comes to you from the wide array of possibilities. Our brains may discount a message that seems illogical (for example, those people who have reported seeing a rose blooming in the snow and knew it was a message from a specific person who loved roses, or knew you loved roses), but notice if it feels meaningful for you. That is the wonder of a spirit communication. After hearing hundreds of spirit message stories like these from clients, family, and friends—it is clear that when we have a personal experience of a message from a loved one in spirit—others' opinions cannot discount how we cherish the message and how we feel regarding this personal "hello."

Chapter 17

Spirit Guides Hard at Work for Us

A spirit guide is always by our side. Let's start by looking at some specific examples. Then I'll share more about how they differ from your departed loved ones in spirit and also answer other frequently asked questions ("FAQs"). Also, consider working with your spirit guide, combined with the Law of Attraction, as you read an example of this in Chapter 10 (the "Action … my Saab Story" portion) to possibly bring more of what you hope for into your life.

Spirit Guide Safety: Easy Does It

Here are two examples of my receiving direct messages from my spirit guides: one where I didn't listen and another where I didn't listen initially, but quickly got the message! Even after having earlier experiences with spirit guides (as in Chapter 10), a medium can get an intuition or message from them and either note it fully, or still brush it to the side. It's a process to come to grips with the fact that our spirit guides are really there for us, and to learn to listen to their messages. I had my own personal journey with this process—as you've read about—as well.

Sharing this first example with my students, I joke that this was the *last time* I didn't listen to my guides when they gave me a clear message. Ever since this experience, I always try to listen and follow the guidance … no matter if it seems inconvenient. For example, if I need to turn right to get home, and I clearly hear my guides telling me to turn left … I do. This may seem silly to some, but it's proven invaluable to me many times.

It was a beautiful, sunny day one January and I was zipping south on Highway 101 to meet a friend and drop off a ton of papers that needed to be shredded. I was excited to lose about 20 to 30 pounds of paper that day! I was cruising along, thinking how good it would feel to drop off all this stuff. As I drove, I clairaudiently heard (in my head), "speeding ticket." It was said evenly, flatly, and without emotion in a male voice. So I knew it was my spirit guide and not my own intuition … which comes to me as more of a gut feeling or just knowing. I heard those two words, looked at my speedometer, and thought, *Nah, I'm good!* I blew off the information. I hadn't had a speeding ticket since I was in my very early twenties and didn't think I was at risk.

I dropped off the paper for shredding and continued along, feeling lighter and full of optimism. The sun was glorious, and the radio was blaring an especially fun song. I was zooming over the hills, happy and singing loudly, with the windows wide open. At some point, I became aware of a police car with its siren blaring that pulled up quickly behind me. I flashed to the warning from earlier that morning ("speeding ticket"). I was going to get my first speeding ticket in a zillion years. Ugh! That was an expensive lesson that I don't need to learn twice. Now I always listen to spirit guide messages and follow through. Perhaps why I didn't listen is I kind of wrote off this message thinking it would not happen to me. After it did, I really knew that I wanted to listen to all the helpful information I was being told by my spirit guides!

Another time I was given a helpful message from my spirit guides was on a getaway to Lake Tahoe. I'd been fortunate to keep in touch with a friend who had a condominium ("condo") at one of the ski resorts there, and she'd been kind enough to rent the place to me several times over the years in the skiing off-season. So, I was up there with a friend in the late summer for a little break from working.

The night after we arrived, I headed out to the workout facility on my own at dusk (as my friend wanted to stay home and get dinner going). As I zoomed up the hill, I made a mental note to get the road-trip snacks out of the car later, because you are not supposed to leave food in cars up in the mountains to tempt the hungry critters. We had some junk food in the car—not my usual fare, but c'mon, it was a road trip—which we forgot to take out when we unpacked upon arrival.

The workout was enjoyable, and I drove slowly back to the condo, feeling especially relaxed thanks to a decadent hot-tub dip (that I only could take advantage of when I visited here). The darkness of night was pierced only by my car headlights, and I noticed there were no parking lot lights at all near the condo. Once the sun went over the mountains, it was *totally* black outside. Since I didn't bring a flashlight and forgot to turn on the condo porch light, I was grateful that I had the walk to the condo memorized.

It was about a 25-foot walk from the car to a short staircase up, and then another 20 feet on a sidewalk to the condo stairs. I parked the car and grabbed the half-eaten bag of barbecued potato chips to bring them inside. I was munching a few as I walked through the pitch-black cool air, and then I heard the dumpster top slam down with a loud clang. I thought, absentmindedly, *Oh someone's taking out their garbage,* and walked toward the dumpsters and the staircase, as that was the direction toward the condo.

I heard a message clairaudiently, "Get back in the car!" It was somewhat stern. I stopped in my tracks for a second, holding a potato chip near my mouth, but then I thought, *Nah, I'm fine.* I kept walking in the dark, straining to see the person who just threw out their garbage with that loud dumpster top clang. But my eyes could not adjust to the darkness … there was no light at all.

I kept walking toward the dumpster and first staircase. Suddenly, I heard in a louder, more stern, male voice: "GET - BACK - IN - THE - CAR!"

I thought *Something must be really wrong!* Then I scrambled to retrace my steps in the dark and fumbled to find the car door. The keys were jumping around in my adrenalin-filled hands, and I struggled to find where the lock was, let alone fit the key into the lock. Once I got the door open, I leapt into the car, slammed the door behind me then quickly locked the doors … all the while in complete darkness.

I didn't know what the warning was about, but my heart was pounding out of my chest as I turned on the ignition and the barbecued chips fell out from under my arm. I turned on the headlights and slowly headed the car in the direction of the dumpster … trying to see where that loud clanging noise came from.

There, next to the dumpster … right in the path where I needed to walk toward the first staircase to the condo … was the biggest black bear I had ever seen!

More adrenaline shot through my body. *Oh my G …*, I was about to walk right into that hungry bear in the pitch-black night with barbecued potato chips in my hands! My heart was now pounding even more fiercely, as I sped away from being a large appetizer for the bear. My tires spun and I raced toward the only place I could think of going … the firehouse across the street. I rang the bell there, and the firefighters let me come inside, a little amused to see the terror of a city girl.

I called my friend in the condo, who sounded a little miffed that I was still gone, because dinner was ready. I breathlessly told her I'd almost walked into a black bear right outside our door. She didn't really seem to get what I'd just been through as she said, with almost childlike wonder, "I want to see it!" as if this was some kind of fun event!

I asked her if she could stand by the condo door to let me in, as some guys from the ski resort came down to escort me into the house. They were great. It was like a scene from a television movie, as the two men brandished their guns (with rubber bullets … I don't know?) and ran up the stairs with their flashlights swooping in every direction, looking for the bear. They barked out orders to me, "All clear! Get in the house!"

My friend did help me quickly get in the door. She continued to talk over dinner about how she'd wished she'd been part of my adventure. I handed her the bag of potato chips, in a daze, needing to unwind after that experience.

My guides clearly "had my back" (and my front!) that evening. I was glad they persisted by repeating their message and being so stern and loud, so I could understand I was clearly in danger and act to help myself.

I'm very grateful for all the times my spirit guides have kept me from getting seriously hurt. These are just a few of the stories throughout my life where my guides came through clearly to help me. There are several other examples. It's a family joke that there have been several times I nearly died, and was miraculously saved. I seem to be like a cat with nine lives, but since I've used up several of them already … I had better lead a quiet life from here on out!

Nocturnal Healers: Let's Get Physical

Here are some accounts where I experienced spirit guides working on requests for physical healing. All of these were especially amazing to me. This first account of spirit guide healing was written by my spouse. My spouse's spirit guides used me (while I was sleeping!) to assist in physical healing.

"During the day, I had been suffering with a horrible sinus headache. Despite trying to get relief from the pain with aspirin and hot shower steam, I was still hoping for relief by nighttime as the pain persisted. In the middle of the night, when we were fast asleep, I was awakened. I felt two of your (Kay's) fingers softly touching my forehead.

I opened my eyes and could see and hear you (Kay) snoring while sleeping. So I was in disbelief as to how you could be touching my face. Lying on your back with your left arm crossing your body, your fingers pushed on the exact spot of my pain … slightly above my eyebrow! Your fingers then applied a little more pressure at the perfect angle to go right at the pain source.

I realized there was some sort of healing going on, so I tried to relax and close my eyes. As I did, I recalled two other times I saw your spirit guides helping you heal while you slept. After about five minutes of the pressure from your fingers—I believe applied by my spirit guides and/or yours by using your arm and hand—I felt like I'd had enough, so I touched your forearm and said "thank you" out loud, softly. Incredibly, your arm then retracted back to your left side and you continued sleeping deeply. The best part of this story is, I woke up the next morning without a headache and felt great! I was so grateful!

The next morning, I remember asking you if you recalled what happened during the night. You (Kay) said something like, 'What … did we have a rain storm outside and I didn't wake up to hear it?' After I told you what happened, you kept asking me to tell you it again … over and over … your eyes were wide with disbelief. I repeated it a few times, each time with more detail. It really happened, and I'll never forget it!"

Here is another instance of healing during the night that I never would have known about had it not been for my spouse. Goodness knows what else is happening whenever I'm alone, snoring away!

Like the healing above, I asked for healing through thought. My heart needed healing, so I requested help from my spirit guides fervently then drifted off to sleep.

The next morning, my spouse again asked, "Do you remember what happened during the night?" I asked, "No, what happened?!"

My spouse reported that one of my arms went up over my head (palm facing the ceiling). Then, my hand and arm moved down a few inches over my face and neck—all while I was dead asleep, breathing heavily, and lightly snoring (attractive, I know). Just past my throat, my hand slowly flipped over so my palm faced down as it moved to rest about an inch over my heart. My hand stayed there—right over my heart—for several minutes.

It amazed me that I asked for help and healing, and it happened! I shared a lot of gratitude for my spirit guides the next day, and now try to remember to do this often.

I also learned that I received healing even when I *didn't ask* for help, as in this next example. Probably from working out or something, my shoulder had been bothering me. In this case, my guides just went to work to heal it, without me knowing.

It's a good thing I sleep so soundly because waking up and experiencing what I'm writing about here would be odd. Again, thanks to the eyewitness (my spouse), I was told that while I was sleeping on my side, my bent arm was going up and down (with my elbow going up toward the ceiling, then moving down to my side, over and over) at the shoulder joint. This was the shoulder that was giving me the pain and trouble! I felt better the next day. My shoulder was not completely healed, but it was better and I appreciated this help as I slept!

I wonder how many other evenings something like this happened, and I didn't even know about it. It's kind of wild to me that I never would have found out about any of this healing if I'd been single. Without the concrete examples, and matching them up with my actual mental requests in the form of thoughts, I probably would not say this is possible. However, after several experiences with this, I thought it might be helpful to share these examples of healing.

Having experienced these events above, I now actively invite my guides to help me by being specific about what I'm wanting help with, and giving them permission to help so they know they are welcome. I'm not sure if others receive this kind of direct healing, but I am hopeful my examples encourage you that spirit guides can be aware of what you are going through. I try to work with my spirit guides daily, and remember to speak to them respectfully and gratefully … just like they are regular people (because they once were).

A Network: Spirit Guide Speed Dial

Like in other chapters, this story begins with me in bed again. One morning, I was awakened very early with a start, hearing a message clairaudiently that something was wrong with my sister, who lived a few states to the east. I thought, *Oh no … I wonder what's wrong?!*

I waited until a decent hour to call my sister and I recall I got her voicemail, so left a message—trying not to sound alarmed. In turn, she left me a voicemail saying she was about to board the airplane to visit our siblings in the Midwest. I kept going over the early morning message I received just as I woke up, since I know those—in my case—tend to be very accurate. My spirit guides like to zing messages in to me early before I'm fully awake and my left brain might discount them. My mind reeled with possibilities, since my sister was flying that day, and I had a nerve-wracked morning, since I couldn't reach her as she was in flight. All I could do was send good thoughts for a safe flight … which I did, repeatedly.

I didn't hear from my sister, and figured she must have landed by now, so I called my other sister's house and heard her sunny voice, "Hi Kay!," as she went on with newsy updates. Finally, I blurted out, "Did her plane land … is she there yet?!" To this, she calmly said, "Yes, she's been here for about a half hour …" and went on with what they were up to. I sighed, like the deflating of a huge hot air balloon. Then, I asked if I could speak with my traveling sister.

She got on the line and sounded like she was having fun with everyone back there. After a minute of her updates, I couldn't stand it anymore! I had to ask her if anything happened today and explained, "I was awakened with an early-morning message (from my spirit guides or maybe even your spirit guides) that you were in trouble! Was the flight bad … were there mechanical difficulties … what happened today?!"

She paused for a second, probably taken aback by all this questioning. She said, "No, the flight was OK." I repeated, "I got this message early this morning that there was something wrong and you kind of needed me. I didn't want to scare you at the airport as we traded messages, but didn't know what this warning was about!"

She finally said, "Ooohh!" I said, "What?!" She said, with a laugh, "I was concerned about those new security screeners at the airports now … you know the ones where they can see you naked under all your clothes? Well, I didn't really want to go through one of those, so I asked my spirit guides to call on all the help I could possibly get." She added, "I guess they called you …" and I could hear her immediately start to tell my other sister what had happened.

Apparently she was so afraid of being seen naked by the airport screener people that she told me later she stood in her living room at the crack of dawn that day and shouted up toward her ceiling, "All right, you spirit people! I need lots of help today!" So my guides, or her guides, or both, followed through by calling me (clairaudiently), so to speak. After holding so much tension and concern, I surrendered to the hilarity of the whole thing.

As it turns out, my sister did get her help. She didn't have to go through the new security body scanner at the airport. So I guess her request worked after all! This is an example of how spirit guides hear us and do their best to help where they can get a message through (whether or not the message is crystal clear to us).

More on Spirit Guides

After reading my personal accounts on some of the ways spirit guides can hear and respond to our requests (whether conscious or unconscious), you may have questions about spirit guides and how to begin working with them. What I've come to know about spirit guides is mainly through what I have experienced with them firsthand. While I am not an expert on spirit guides, here is some helpful information that seems to be true for me, after picking up an amalgam of information about guides while in lectures, classes, and workshops with reputable mediums as well as hearing radio programs by various mediums. Please note: I do not profess to be an expert on spirit guides so I share this information below as just something to consider. Feel free to research more about spirit guides on your own.

Q: What is a spirit guide, and how are they different from an angel?

In short, a spirit guide has been a human being before and an angel never has. Both can aid us in our life. So, we have both a spirit guide and also angels to assist us. Angels are said to attend to different needs in the universe, including protecting us. There are several orders of angels: seraphim, cherubim, thrones, dominations, virtues, powers, principalities, archangels, and angels. Like spirit guides, we do not necessarily need to be aware of them (or even believe in them, for that matter) to be assisted by them.

From what I've come to learn, a spirit guide has developed to such a point that they have enough spiritual and/or emotional knowledge to aid us in this lifetime. Like humans, spirit guides are continuing to learn, grow, and mature. A master spirit guide is said to be someone we've known before in other lifetimes and we agreed to have them as our guide before we came into this life. The function of a spirit guide is to protect, assist, and guide us through this lifetime.

It's important to note that spirit guides are just that … guides. They are there to try to *guide* us through our life, whether we are aware of them or not. Because they are guides, they may not give us all the answers or answer everything we want to know. Their job is to guide, and some things we need to decide on our own and live out (and yes, they may give us guidance on those things, but may not directly tell us what to do). Even if they do, it's still up to us to work through what makes sense for us to do in this life as we are the ones deciding and living with the consequences. It can be part of our work in this lifetime to figure out what to do, or what decision to make … whether we receive their guidance or not.

Q: Do we all have at least one spirit guide?

From what I've been taught … yes, we all have at least one spirit guide (whether we can hear their guidance or not). It's suggested that some in the healing professions (or possibly others who need them) have more than one spirit guide.

Q: Have I known my spirit guide in this lifetime (are they departed loved ones)?

From what I've come to learn, the master guide is not anyone you knew in this lifetime (but you may have known them in other lifetimes). If you have a departed loved one from this lifetime who wants to be on your spirit guide team to help you, they can request to do that and join your team (this may be for a period of time though). For example, I was told by a medium who was giving me an evidential reading (that is, it contained provable facts, so I knew he was connecting with a particular departed loved one … in this case, my aunt, a former nun) that my aunt wanted to be on my spirit guide team to help with my mediumship readings. This was in the early years of my development circle training, and later she fulfilled her help (I was so grateful for her offer). In later years, I was told that I was being given a new spirit guide to help me with mediumship readings, who had a more advanced level of expertise in assisting mediums. I'm grateful to both of them.

Q: What are different types of spirit guides?

I've heard of many different kinds of spirit guides. Here are some of the most consistent I've learned about from various sources.

Master Guide—We all have this guide … and some may have other types of guides. The master guide can be thought of as someone we have known before in other lifetimes that we agreed would guide us through this particular lifetime. If you have a few guides, this master guide is like the director of them all, or—if you like—the quarterback (or CEO) of the team. Our master guide tries to give us messages through our dream or waking state (messages that feel like a coincidence, synchronicity, or our own intuition … even though it's really coming from our guides and we cannot yet discern the difference between our guides' messages and our own intuition).

Gatekeeper—Whether you are a medium or not, a gatekeeper guide is to protect you from energies that might cause you harm. This guide is especially important to mediums who work to connect people here with their departed loved ones who have crossed over to the other side.

Many mediums work with a gatekeeper guide that allows spirit people (departed loved ones of our clients) in one by one, so we know who is speaking to us. The gatekeeper guide also assists to just let through the departed loved ones for our particular client (and not others, as it's very important a medium not open to just anyone in spirit). The gatekeeper helps a medium connect with departed spirits for our clients, and can also assist us—if we ask—in the event it's difficult for us to hear, see, or sense a piece of information the departed spirit loved one is trying to convey to us for our client.

This guide also helps a medium when departed loved ones (perhaps without a client appointment) try to get through to the medium as they sleep, in hopes of passing a message on to someone here on earth. It can help if the medium asks for assistance from his or her guide so random spirits cannot get through while she is sleeping. That way the medium can rest properly.

There are many other types of spirit guides a person may have, such as: a medical (or healing) guide, who helps with our health or physical healing; a relationship or career guide (or both), who is assigned to help you with a specific aspect of your life for a period of time, or ongoing; a helper guide, who sees what we are wanting to learn according to our interests and attracts—with the help of the Law of Attraction—the kind of guide that can help us. An example of this final spirit guide for me is the gatekeeper guide that helps me with my mediumship readings every day.

Q: How can I tell the difference between my own intuition and the messages of a spirit guide?

If you are just starting with this kind of information, you may not be able to tell the difference at this time. This is not unusual, or anything to feel badly about. It took me quite some time to discern the difference. Sometimes we feel connected to our intuition or spirit guides' messages. Sometimes we don't, early on. Initially, I started to note what felt like intuitions, or gut feelings, or things I just knew but I didn't know how I knew.

This can all be seen as clairsentience. Over time, I started to hear (as I'm clairaudient) the messages from my spirit guides that felt different than my own intuition.

Intuition often comes as a flash of information, or an impression, or an emotion, out the blue. It can have a physical location, as in a gut feeling, or something just popping into your head. I feel my gut feelings in my solar plexus area (below the heart but above the navel, just below the rib cage in the center of the body). However, it's important to note that some of my students feel intuition in another part of their body than I do … it's very individual. At first, recognizing intuition will allow you to distinguish it from spirit guides over time. The difference may not be clear to you in the beginning, so be patient with this process of getting to know your guides, as you may be developing the relationship with them for quite a while before you actually sense or hear them. It's a different process for everyone.

Spirit guides can have their own way of saying things, in their own tone, and with their own emotion. If their emotional tone is different than yours, you can easily use this as a way to see it's not your intuition; it may be a message from your guide. You'll see this in the example above in this chapter, where I note I was relaxed and happy (after the Lake Tahoe work out) when my spirit guides were pretty stern and demanding (telling me to "Get back in the car!"), just before I nearly ran into a hungry bear in the dark night.

Also, my guides will use phrasing that is clearly not mine. They think and talk differently than I do. So, I might hear something from them like, "Follow the light that illuminates your path …" or something more practical, but still in their language, like, "You have been assigned to …". I don't think or speak this way, so it's clear to me when I'm hearing unusual phrasing that it's my spirit guide (and not my thought). Similarly, when I'm doing a reading and the client's spirit guide comes through, they all have different personalities and ways of speaking. Like I said, it's like meeting different people at a party, and it's pretty remarkable! One clear indicator of a spirit guide is when you hear a male voice and you're a woman, or vice versa.

Even with all this information, you may still not yet believe in spirit guides. Believe me, I used to be there myself. Now, after developing quite a relationship with my own guides, I have countless, fun examples of provable messages from spirit guides for somewhat skeptical clients during my readings. One of my favorites was with a client who was a kind man, large in stature, and clearly did not believe in spirit guides when I brought up the subject. But he was polite and listened to their messages. After I shared a key event from his childhood via his spirit guides, he jerked back in his chair and said, "Nobody knows about that!" Then, he sat forward, looked intently into my eyes and said, "Who did you say these spirit guides are?!"

Q: How can I work with my spirit guide (or guides)?

Your spirit guides are ready and waiting to guide. There are examples above where I talk about the Law of Attraction, protecting in times of danger, and even enlisting others to help. The examples you come to learn personally about your spirit guides may be different than mine, but the key points in working with spirit guides seem to me to be: asking for help, being specific about what you want, giving them permission to help, or assist, and expressing gratitude to them. Whether you hear, sense, or follow their gentle guidance or not, it seems to me to be important to speak to spirit guides respectfully and thank them. If you were a guide to a specific person for their entire lifetime, and you were never acknowledged or thanked, how would that be? I send gratitude when I think of it, and I enjoy starting my day with gratitude for my spirit guides after I awaken (before even getting out of bed). It's also calming to do this again before sleeping. Just entertaining the thought that your guide is really there, and then starting the conversation, is a good beginning to developing a relationship.

If you want to take the relationship a step further, it can be helpful to provide your spirit guide with clear and specific information on what you are trying to bring into your life. Also, get clear on your intention and share that thought with your guide as well. You can, for example, invite your guide to help you bring in a specific item, or kind of relationship. To illustrate how important being specific is, if you heard a friend ask, "Can you get me something at the store?" you would have no idea what she meant. Same goes for spirit guides. It would be so much clearer to say, "Can you please get me a quart of 1 percent milk at the grocery store?"

So, rather than being vague, be specific. Instead of thinking, "Gosh, I hate my job schedule," try something more specific as in, "I would like a job from 8:00 a.m. to 3:00 p.m., so that I am home in time to see my children." If I can't get that exactly, "I would love to have a boss that would be open to my working a flexible schedule, so I could work more on certain days to make up for going to pick up my kids from school."

Asking for the *essence* of what you want seems to be important, as well as not being completely tied to the outcome (as in, what comes to you, or how). Of course, you have free will, so you can accept or reject what comes to you. In my own experience (using the Saab story from Chapter 10 above), if a perfectly good car came to me that I asked for, I would be flexible on some of the features (say, I wouldn't reject it just because the interior color wasn't exactly the shade I was hoping for). The same is true for relationships. Feel free to ask for the essence of who, or what, you hope for … then be flexible if you can, to determine if the person who comes your way is good for you or at least workable.

Remember to get clear on what you want and your intention. If you just ask for a relationship, your guide doesn't know exactly what kind you prefer. I've heard some clients share that they want a committed relationship, while others have had different things they have asked for, including some who truthfully share that they hope for a more fun, casual dating relationship at this point in their life. As for your intention, will you date anyone who comes your way who seems interested? Or, is your intention more clear, as in some variation of what YOU want? "I want a committed, healthy relationship in the Chicago area or surrounding suburbs." This way, your guide knows what you want, where and your intention is clear (look into the Law of Attraction for more on manifesting).

It's also seems to be important to take practical steps toward what you want, whether or not you can see evidence of your guides helping you with what you want. This isn't magic. Yes, you have an equal role to play in manifesting. Your spirit guides are helping you manifest but this takes work on your part (and the wonderful body of work on the Law of Attraction includes just how important our thoughts and emotions complement all this as well). Think through the practical steps of what you need to do to bring in what you want, and then do them. Manifesting is active! It can be fun to experiment with how this works for you.

When what you want shows up, will you follow through and let yourself have it? In all these examples I share, I had to do my work to make it happen, then I had to find the courage to allow it in, or receive. How many of us see examples of a friend getting what she says she wants—like a great job or a beautiful romance—and then she self-sabotages the situation. See where you are about allowing yourself to receive what you want. If you need help with that part, find a good therapist or life coach to explore where you may be getting hung up.

Q: Do you work with a client's spirit guides in a reading?

Yes! In my role as a medium, I am honored to see spirit guides come through for people all the time. Again, we each have our own guide(s). Jane's (a hypothetical client) spirit guides come through for her because they know what she is thinking, what she is hoping for, and what she is worried about, and more. Jane's guides address much of this and she validates it, then knows she isn't alone … her guides are there to help her. Time and time again, I witness spirit guides coming through with specific content so clients know they are there for them.

If a client wants a mediumship reading to hear from their loved ones in spirit, oftentimes their spirit guides pop in at the beginning also. Let's face it, if you were a master spirit guide to a human being for their entire life, and your human didn't know you existed … wouldn't you want to use the voice of the medium to say a few things to this human you are with for their life span? If I were that master spirit guide, I'm sure I would!

No one taught me how to share spirit guides' messages in a reading with a client. I just started doing it. It's become one of my specialties, to introduce clients to their spirit guide. A spirit guide can give guidance on what a client could do about a particular situation, but—as with anything—they are only guides. Each client is solely responsible for determining what is in their best interest. We are the ones making the decisions and living with the consequences that follow. So it's important that clients decide what seems right for them, as we have free will.

Q: How are a spirit guide's messages different from our own internal chatter voice?

Spirit guides only say kind, loving, or helpful information … or issue a kind of "heads up" or warning, with the hope of helping you in the long run. A spirit guide *does not* sound like the "internal chatter" voice in our head. Spirit guides are never negative, chastising, or mean. They may warn you (as in, "Kay, get your car tires checked") because they are trying to help keep you safe, or help you in the long run. But they will not judge or criticize you. For example, they would not say, "Kay, you are such a horrible driver … I cannot believe you ruined your tire … get it fixed!"

Spirit guides are benevolent and helpful, even if they need to share a warning, as in the real example above with my car tire … I got the tires checked on a Thursday and there was a nail in one of them, so I got it fixed. I thus avoided a blowout or a flat tire on the freeway the next day (and wasting about 2-3 hours … or getting my hands and clothes really dirty), as I had to drive 50 miles to teach a class. If you hear a mean or critical voice, it may more likely be your own mental chatter or internalized negative messages people said to you in your younger years (or possibly other sources, such as with schizophrenics hearing voices). I am *not* discussing schizophrenia in this book … for that, please get help from the appropriate mental health professional or request a referral from your medical provider.

Q: What is the Law of Attraction?

Some of you may be familiar with the Law of Attraction, a way to understand and work with the concept of like attracts like. That is, what we are thinking and feeling emotionally is connected to what is coming into our life (so, to use a quick example, it can be more helpful to think about what we want versus what we do not want … for example, think about abundance if you wish for that, not its opposite). The Law of Attraction is different from our spirit guides (but it can be used to make the working with your spirit guides more powerful as you work with manifesting what you hope for).

The Law of Attraction is just one of the universal laws to learn and use to assist you in trying to manifest what you desire (be it a relationship, a job, or something else). You can read more about the other laws that go hand in hand with the Law of Attraction, which is considered one of the more powerful laws. There is so much information available online on the Law of Attraction, or at your favorite book or audio source.

Q: How can I work with my spirit guides to try to enhance the Law of Attraction?

Both our spirit guides and the Law of Attraction are extremely powerful forces in and of themselves. Combining learning about, or working with, both—in my opinion—may create a powerful synergy. Here are a few tips on how to help spirit guides help you (see also the detailed section above on "How can I work with my spirit guide?").

First, give your spirit guides permission to work with you. You can do this (even if you don't quite believe in them just yet) by simply thinking or saying that you invite them to send you helpful information about your life in whatever way they can. It may come in a sleep, or a waking, state. You may feel like you have a new idea or direction after you receive their message. You may receive a synchronicity (what I used to call a coincidence) that gets your attention. Or they may communicate in another way. These messages can sometimes be subtle, so have your antennae out. You don't have to talk to them out loud, but some people like to do that, which is fine. You can simply "think at them" and invite them in. Learning more about the Law of Attraction from the plentiful source of books, video, or audio is a great way to put this to work along with working with your spirit guide.

Q: Do I have to know if my spirit guide is female or male, or know their name, to begin working with them?

This is a very popular question from my clients. The answer is no. While all spirits are actually more androgynous (as a soul), they do feel female, or male, to me. So, you do not need to know if your guide is female or male, nor do you need to know their name before beginning to work with them. It's not uncommon to not know this information for years (or some may never feel or sense this information ... it's ok). What's most important is that you begin to share your requests with them if you like (by simple thought is fine, unless you prefer to say it out loud). Also, I think it's valuable to acknowledge that they are trying to help you, and share your thanks and gratitude with them on a regular basis, or when you remember to. You can thank them each morning after you wake up, or at a certain time each day (just as a simple way to remember to do it). Over time, you may feel or know more about your guide (you could even meditate then ask them about themselves), but if you don't ... it's enough to simply send your thoughts their way. If a name comes to you for them, great. If not, don't worry about it at all.

I hope this chapter illuminates some of the ways our spirit guides can work with us, and how you can begin to develop more of a relationship with your guide.

Chapter 18

Love Never Dies (Neither Do People's Spirits)

Beginning with my journey after my near-death experience (NDE) until the time of this writing, I can see how a kind of pattern emerged in my development that continued to pull me toward assisting those in spirit and those who want to hear from their loved ones in spirit. From being unaware of being "different" in my early twenties right after the NDE, and then starting that journey (complete with the wonderful helpers I met along the way, and my trying my best to ignore my opponents as I was drawn along my new path), it dawned on me that layer upon layer was being built upon as I went along, doing my studying, practicing, and training.

I had inklings of this when I was well into my journey of studying mediumship, after the earlier premonitions and psychic knowings, and now it's easier for me to see clearly that I needed layers of learning and skills to become a medium. While I didn't realize it as I was going through the years trying to gain the skills ... I now see that each layer built upon the foundation of the previous one. It reminded me of a pyramid.

The bottom layer of the pyramid needs to be wide and long, so that the next layer can dovetail nicely onto it. Then, I needed still more layers of skills, as well as actual experiences, as I've come to learn that we don't seem to believe in metaphysical experiences until we actually have a felt sense of one. Even a prior skeptic often believes, after having a felt sense of something paranormal happening (for example, a dream visitation from a parent, or other loved one, in spirit).

The layers of the pyramid, I imagine, are early psychic and premonition experiences, followed by being in graduate school to learn to sit with someone who is grieving intensely (as many of my clients naturally are). The mediumship emerged only after these first layers were well in place. The next layer was substantial, years of reading about mediumship, as well as ongoing practice in development circles, classes, workshops, and having those important direct experiences receiving and giving spirit messages.

In addition to the wealth of knowledge from development circle leaders over the years, the next layer was study with world-renowned mediums from whom I could learn more about how to best serve spirit and clients. And, finally, a leap of faith to change careers entirely and give readings more than just nights and weekends, but full-time. To mix my metaphors, the icing on the cake (I mean, pyramid) is teaching students who want to learn more about their own intuitive, psychic, and mediumship skills—along with giving one-on-one readings to my wonderful clients—as these are both very rewarding parts of my journey.

Below you will find just a few examples of what clients can receive from a mediumship reading. A whole other book could be shared about readings that I have permission from clients to write about (all other readings are confidential, of course). However, I tried to simply choose several readings from one family below. First, I'll share how you can get the most from your reading using your own energy and beliefs.

Some readings are more healing in sync with what the spirit person wants to say, along with emotions shared, like apologies, gratitude, or other emotions. Readings should also include evidential (provable) information that is recognized as specific to the spirit person (or can be checked with a relative, or friend). While all readings should include evidential information, the person in spirit often cares more about sharing heartfelt healing messages versus those hearing the reading wanting to know it's really from a particular person of course.

It's my job to walk the tightrope in a reading and keep balancing both types of messages and information. Some people in spirit will tell me clairaudiently that evidential information is not why they are coming through, and then go on to share their messages they want to say with their loved one. While nearly all spirit people will talk about provable information, I sometimes actually hear spirit person say to me, "I don't really want to talk about how I got sick and why I died." while they go on to other messages *they* want to say.

How a reading goes is also based on the client. Some are very open and remark, "Whatever is said is what I need to hear." But most people coming for a reading ask for provable details (I understand that personally, from wanting to hear from my mother and others in spirit). The person in spirit is working hard to change their vibration to match the slower, denser energy of our world (as I am raising my vibration to better hear them). I try my best to serve the client sitting in front of me and am also serving the person in spirit speaking.

Hope, excitement, and nervousness are often present when most clients start a reading. This energy is palpable in my clients. As I bring them information, often I can visibly see (or hear, in a phone reading) a client relaxing within the first 10 minutes of a one-hour reading. Their earlier excitement and understandable "nerves" fade into being completely engaged in the conversation with their own personal spirit guide, as they hear information they can relate to then start to understand their spirit guide is really with them in their life. As their energy shifts to this more relaxed state, it is actually easier for me to bring through clearer information … because the spirit is using the energy not only of the medium, but of the client as well.

So, to receive the most clear, heartfelt, and provable messages—try to be the client who believes in mediumship and is relaxed and open (with bonus points if you are feeling warm or loving emotions as spirit people can more easily come in on this higher vibration). It's understandable that people are excited and nervous before a reading, because the unknown can be nerve-wracking … for anyone. A client (or "sitter") who relaxes and opens into the reading process actually receives a better reading. So, maybe it would be good to have clients go for a massage, a workout, or even meditate before a reading. I'm joking, but it probably would help.

If a person is skeptical yet open to the mediumship process, they can be more difficult to read than the hypothetical client above. I joke with my self-identified skeptical clients, "Try to tell yourself that you believe in this ... just for this one hour," as their belief can make their reading go better. Some laugh when I say this, but their more positive belief, and level of openness can change how their reading goes. Skeptical people can be read and receive a reading though, I just mention these points if these people want to try a reading.

Can you guess how a reading goes for a person who does not believe that spirit communication can occur? Peoples' thoughts do seem to create their reality. When I share the messages coming through from their loved ones, and friends, in spirit, I can energetically feel the messages bouncing off a kind of perimeter around them and sadly ricocheting over to the side, unreceived. This is most apparent when, say, two siblings (or a couple) want to attend a reading together, and I can feel the messages being received by one of them at one end of the couch. Yet, I can feel the messages kind of bounce off the other person. In one such reading, the sibling who was receiving their messages explained by email afterward that their sister didn't believe in mediumship but wanted to come check it out anyway.

Each reading varies quite a bit, based on the spirit person's unique personality and level of communication skills from the other side, where the client is (as I note above), and of course, the particular medium. Spirits who are newly crossed over need to learn how to get their ideas across to a medium. Spirits also know how open their loved one (my client) is to this process. Sometimes, it's humorous, as I say to a client, "Your mom tells me you don't really believe in this," and then the client laughs knowingly.

Some messages heard in a reading can surprise a client as they may not know the information first hand. The person in spirit knows what they are trying to say … and hopefully the client makes a connection during the message—but often the understanding happens *after* a reading, when the client has time to reflect and connect the dots. So while the sender (the spirit person) and the receiver (the client) can connect about the message, I am more like the radio or telephone that conveys the message.

At times, if I ask, I can tune in to find out what the message is about if the client does not understand it the first time. Often, a client will call or email me after a reading, explaining that they now understand a message after they checked with a relative, or friend, who helped verify information. Other times, a client will connect with the information the medium conveys from the spirit person right away, and blurt out, "Did he really just say that?!" Some burst out laughing as they realize that the person in spirit is cracking an inside joke; at other times, tears flow as they feel the love (or an apology) coming from their spirit loved one.

All readings are confidential, but below are a few examples of readings that I have permission from the clients to share with you. I hope you enjoy "sitting in" on these readings.

A mother requested a telephone reading for her son, Max, as a gift. From the start, I was so delighted by his warm and open manner. Max gave me permission to share this one tidbit from early on in his reading.

It was early on a Thursday evening when Max and I talked for the first time. I said first that I had a woman in spirit coming through, then identified her as his grandmother (then later as his maternal grandma), as well as other identifying information. I was a little puzzled by something I saw clairvoyantly (in my mind's eye).

This grandma showed herself as the spitting image of the long-time late actress Jessica Tandy. I was pretty sure (though not yet positive, until I asked him) that his grandma was *not* actually Jessica Tandy. So, I described to him that she showed herself AS Jessica Tandy. Spirit people show mediums details to get you to identify something about them (though the recipient will get what it is—hopefully eventually, if not in the moment). So, if the client does not get the connection, the medium might say … did your grandma looked like an actress, or was she an actress herself, or was her name Jessica … to try and help the client make the connection the spirit person is trying to say. A medium can also ask follow up questions to the spirit person to learn more about this reference.

Since I wasn't sure a young man in his early 20s like Max would know who the late actress Jessica Tandy was, I gave him a kind of verbal lead-in to this information. Max's reply to my description of grandma walking out AS Jessica Tandy was a few moments of silence. Then he ventured, "You mean, 'Driving Miss Daisy'?" I laughed unexpectedly, delighted that this young man knew who Jessica Tandy was! I said, "Yes, that's the actress, from that movie … that I am seeing in my mind's eye for you!"

He then explained the back story. As his grandma aged, his mom would drive her around to appointments and on errands. Mother and daughter joked that this was just like scenes from the movie "Driving Miss Daisy."

It was so sweet that grandma didn't come out and just *say*

the movie title to me. Grandma actually *showed* herself as the star of "Driving Miss Daisy," because that was the inside joke. In this way, she was both identifying that it was she and showing her sense of humor with a reference the whole family knew. Spirits can be so charming, clever, and funny! I'm just thrilled that Max allowed me to share this dear story from his reading.

Close to the date of Max's reading, I had my first reading with his mother.

Prior to my reading with Josephine, we'd never met and I knew nothing about her. These kinds of readings are very exciting to me as a medium, as everything that is coming through from spirit is brand-new to me. A medium "worth their salt" does not want to know anything about a client's person, or people, in spirit before the reading because they want to bring that information through. This is more evidential.

I'd begun the reading with Josephine as I do with all clients, asking if she'd had a reading before, whether it was a psychic reading or a mediumship reading (or a combination), and finding out whether that was a positive or negative experience. These answers helped me share what she could expect during our hour together.

My sixty-minute readings often include information from a client's spirit guide and then move into spirit loved ones (or friends) coming through. I started with specific information Josephine's guide shared that she could identify with, that she always "smelled good." I'd learned to get over being embarrassed, as spirits often make me say the darndest things. Josephine laughed and said that she indeed enjoys wearing a favorite perfume when she goes out. She even offered, "People often say to me, 'You smell good.'" Clients will sometimes take a guide's overall information more seriously after sharing a specific detail. Josephine's guides also conveyed that she is so good at creating special holiday gift items that are quite beautiful or delicious, and joked that they'd like to put in their order early!

Next, I started to receive information from Josephine's father in spirit. He shared (after I asked) the health issue he was struggling with before he passed, which she confirmed, then began sharing detailed personal messages that she validated as accurate. Then he changed gears and talked about being on the other side and no longer having a body. He even shocked me a little with his sense of humor saying, "My feet smell better." While spirits still have their memories, personality, and all other qualities of their consciousness, this was just a humorous way he talked about no longer having a body. Josephine confirmed he was a jokester in life.

While her father was coming through, I could feel his affection, warmth and love for Josephine, and I always share this clairsentient information with my client.

Since a reading is a spirit person's big chance to come through, they often jump from one topic to the next in the limited time they are able to lower their vibration to connect on the same wavelength as the human medium (who needs to raise his or her vibration in order to receive the information as they work to get on the same "radio station" if you will). Next, Josephine's father piped up and said he really loved a certain pudding that she made. Josephine said she always made a special Italian pudding for the holidays, and her dad did love it!

Next, Josephine's Dad shared the name of a close friend in spirit. I received "Bill." Josephine said this was a close family friend they called Uncle Bill. I also received "Stan," and she confirmed he was another old friend of the family, now in spirit.

A final message I'll share from her father was nearly lost on me. He was trying to get me to talk about "ducks." I walk by a pond where there are ducks on a "power walk" a few times a week, so I passed it off. I was prepared to drop it as my own thought, but her dad seemed insistent on getting this through to me, screaming in my ear, "QUACK, QUACK!" I thought, *Oh, dear, I really have to say this*, so I said, "What's with the ducks?" She laughed and said her mom had ducks on EVERYTHING in the house: dishes, glassware, towels … you name it! We chuckled at her father's insistence on this evidential piece of information about their family.

No sooner did Josephine's dad finish up his messages with some loving goodbyes than her mother stepped right in to speak through me. Jessica Tandy was back! I asked Josephine's mom how she had passed away. She had a problem in her chest; the medical procedures involved a tube. I asked for more detail and she said to me via clairaudience: "Complications from an infection." I also asked how old she was when she passed; I'll often get a range like, "late 70s to 80s," but her mom zeroed in on 86. Josephine confirmed everything, including that her Mom had died at 86 … what a really great communicator she was, to tell me the actual age she crossed over rather than the age range.

Next, mom empathized that Josephine's name had been "cumbersome" for her at times, to which she exclaimed, "Did she really just say that?!" I got the feeling, clairsentiently, that her name was too long to fit on the forms at school, and too hard to spell for a young child. She also shared with her daughter that she was fine and happy on the other side, to give her some relief from the sadness and grief over her mom's passing.

Before finishing, Josephine's mom said that her grandma would like to say hello. She showed me, clairvoyantly (in my mind's eye), a dessert she used to make, with a specific filling and dough, and Josephine told me the name of the dessert. Finally, Josephine's mother brought the reading to a close with: "I LOVE YOU! Don't fret about me. I'm fine!"

It's easier for those in spirit to want us not to hurt and be sad anymore. But it's hard to just leap beyond the grieving phase. Readings can provide closure, healing, peace, a sense of reconnection, and sometimes, laughter. There is no one "right" way to grieve, and the path is intensely personal. What clients say they get from a reading seems as individual as fingerprints. I don't solicit feedback, but often clients will just call, email, or even text me about what they got out of their reading.

Like many of my readings, if clients are interested in hearing from their personal spirit guide (or guides), I'm happy to bring those messages through near the beginning of the reading, followed by the people they knew in spirit. I've noticed that after one reading, people often ask to just hear from their spirit guides for their next entire reading.

Some clients come to a medium for a reading just once, and others enjoy coming back for a second reading. Josephine did request additional readings for her husband, her son Max, and herself near the holiday season. Some of the same spirits came through, but new relatives popped in as well.

After several personal messages from Josephine's spirit guides that were meant only for her, I'll share some others from her second reading with me to give you more of a flavor of what our spirit guides know and want to say. What spirit guides say is so incredibly different for each client, so this is just one example. Josephine's spirit guides told me, clairaudiently, that she would like to travel. When I asked for more detail, they told about her traveling overseas to countries located near water and I heard, "Scotland." She confirmed that when her husband retired, they hoped to travel to Italy and Scotland as well.

Next, her guides complimented her on a part of her personality, that she could be detail-oriented. They said, "I wouldn't know you if you weren't meticulous," in a good-natured, affectionate way. They were underscoring how she was great in her work career and also in tackling personal projects, adding this message, "Anytime we can be who we really are … it's a good thing!"

As spirit guides seem to know the value, or benefit, of using a human medium's vocal cords to get many messages through within just a few minutes, they jump from topic to topic … as the people we know in spirit (who have crossed over) often do. If they only have a few minutes, or words, they often use phrases, snippets, or one picture that's worth a thousand words as the saying goes.

Next, Josephine's spirit guides told me that she is discovering new, positive aspects of herself at this time of her life. They told me to say, "You are blessed" and gave me the feeling clairsentiently that she can do what many people cannot. When I ran this by her, she said it was about her retirement.

My San Francisco job was in this very field, so I knew how fortunate she was to have reached retirement. I so hoped for that situation for more people and tried to (in my prior career) educate them on how to get there through the quarterly newsletters I helped edit and produce. I joked that she was the poster child for my previous career ... since she had actually figured out how to retire!

The spirit guides talked about her filling her newfound time after retirement with volunteer work. I explained to her that she has 100 percent free will and can do whatever works for her, and she told me that volunteer work was in her plan all along. Next, her guides talked about her knack for seeing what needed to be spruced up or fixed. She confirmed she does that on a regular basis.

Finally, her spirit guides summarized this part of her life by saying to me clairaudiently, "This may be one of the most enjoyable parts of your life. Live it up!" Then, we moved to hearing from the first person in spirit who came through to me for Josephine.

As we changed gears, I said, "I have a female in spirit for you. It is your mother." I can ask what generational level the spirit is on, and they will answer me—grandparent level, parent level, their level (a brother, sister or friend), or younger level (child, or niece or nephew).

My client's mother said, "I'm so happy for you! You've been troubled enough with work ... I'm glad you are free!" She observed that not many people get to be retired today ..."Good for you!" Her mother also said she had diabetes and a problem with her legs, and my client confirmed that.

My client's mother in spirit said that she would like to take Josephine out for dinner and spend some time with her. "We have a lot to catch up on." This was a kind of 'wouldn't it be nice if we could' kind of idea. Josephine was understandably emotional at hearing this invitation. Her mother told me that her own personality from her time on earth was now more blended with her true nature … her soul.

Next, her mother talked about a pet in spirit with her, and my client mentioned their dog that was loved dearly. Her mother went on to say that she did needle work, and my client confirmed that her mother crocheted and embroidered. Also, her mother in spirit accurately showed herself with a few extra pounds on her frame, and my client said that yes, she was heavy.

This spirit returned to the message she wanted to give; she liked that her daughter was generous and warm … and that if she wanted to get something done, she surely would!

I asked her mother in spirit what in particular she knew about her daughter's life and she mentioned a manicure. My client laughed. She does indeed get her nails done on a regular basis … every three to four weeks, and was tickled that her mother could see this.

As I could feel her personality, her mother was a caring and loving person who was comfortable sharing her ideas and opinions. She remarked, "All is fine where I am. I'm glad you looked me up!" (as if to say … thank you for looking in on me and setting up this appointment so we could talk together). She joked about wanting to visit my client here on earth but "… the tickets would be too expensive." Truly, she can look in on her daughter and visit whenever she likes.

She said in closing, "It doesn't end. We go on from here. I love you, dear. Please give a big hug to your family. And enjoy the holidays!"

Later in this reading, this same client had a visit from an unexpected person in spirit. Her cousin introduced himself as someone who died in a car accident. She confirmed that was how he had died. He told her, "Do things while you are young and can enjoy them," that he was really fond of her, that he was grateful that he was allowed to "pop in," to take up some of the time in her reading, and that he felt extremely protective of her. He concluded, "I have thought a lot about you … you are an angel!"

I asked my client what it was like to hear from these people in spirit. She said, "My cousin was a mind-blower! And I love to hear from my mom!"

I want to thank both Josephine and her son, Max, for allowing me to share with you these messages from their loved ones in spirit, from the father with the now good-smelling feet to his lovely wife, who looks like Jessica Tandy! That way you can imagine what a reading is like, if you have never had one. It goes without saying that spirit people capture my heart on a regular basis, along with my clients and their spirit guides. I absolutely *love* being of service to those in spirit and their loved ones here on earth. Often when I say goodbye to clients, I feel as though I've just been at a wonderful dinner party where I met their unique relatives, with each of their personalities shining through.

Thank you for coming along to read about my journey after my near-death experience. As you can see, it took me many years to see how my path had changed. I am so happy to humbly try to fulfill the mission I was given the night I nearly crossed over for good. Simply trying to be of service to others can be a calling in and of itself. Warmest regards to you as you follow your intuition on your own personal journey.

APPENDIX

Quiz on Intuitive Traits

This quiz can simply gauge some of the initial characteristics often found in intuitive people. It is included as a starting point. Results can be improved. Please know that everyone has a measure of intuition, and that it can be developed with any combination of books, classes or workshops (in person or online), regular practice, recorded exercises and meditations to help meet your spirit guide, Internet videos from reputable psychics and/or mediums, and more.

On a separate piece of paper (especially if this is a library book), go through the questions quickly, with pencil or pen. Don't over think your answers!

1. Have you had experiences of "just knowing" things—without knowing exactly how (examples: seeing, hearing, feeling, or otherwise sensing ... without prior knowledge)?
   Yes or No (circle one for each question below)
2. Do you come from a family with ability to "just know" things?*
   Yes or No

3. Are you left-handed, or ambidextrous (use both hands)* for various tasks (such as, writing with your left hand but performing sports with your right hand, or being able to use either hand to write, etc.)?

   Yes or No

4. Do you stay up later in the evening than the average person? Do you sleep less than 7-8 hours per night? Do you have sleep interruptions regularly?*

   Yes or No

5. Do you prefer to spend time alone because it helps you feel replenished?*

   Yes or No

6. Do you feel a need to spend time outside (in nature, if possible) regularly?*

   Yes or No

7. Do you have talent and/or experience in one or more of the arts?*

   Yes or No

8. Do you sometimes transpose (or flip around) numbers or letters* as you hear, think or even write them? For example, if you hear someone say "415" on the phone, do you sometimes write "451" or other combination of these numbers?

   Yes or No

9. Were you an exceptional student?*

   Yes or No

10. Do you have a photographic memory or total recall (are you able to recall information by what it looked like on the page or computer screen)?*

    Yes or No

11. Do you have experience as a mediator (either formally or informally); that is, are you able to see or understand various sides of an issue, and help each side see the other's point of view?*
    Yes or No

12. Are you an only child?*
    Yes or No

13. Do you have trouble detecting when people are not telling the truth? Think of past friends or dating relationships to jog your memory. Or, have you ever considered yourself, or been called, slightly gullible? Are you, by nature, a trusting person? Do you take people "at face value"?
    Yes or No

14. Would you consider yourself a sensitive, or highly sensitive, person?
    Yes or No

15. Do you have an advanced degree in one of the mental health professions?*
    Yes or No

16. Have you experienced receiving information "out of nowhere," as a sudden, unexpected idea, knowing, or even a "flash" of information?
    Yes or No

17. If you do receive information "out of nowhere," do you get a feeling of confidence about it? Do you have emotions that signal you to retain the information or to believe it is good information?
    Yes or No

18. Have you ever seen an image or picture in a dream, or the flash of an image or symbol (in your mind's eye) during your waking state, which turned out to be helpful in your life?

    Yes or No

19. Have you ever heard a sound or words during your sleeping or waking state in your own voice or another's voice, which turned out to be helpful in your life?

    Yes or No

20. Have you ever felt something that you just knew to be true, without knowing how you knew it?

    Yes or No

21. Have you ever smelled something so real but looked around and knew there was nothing in your immediate area with that kind of smell?

    Yes or No

22. Have you ever tasted something so real, but knew you had not eaten anything with that taste in the last several hours?

    Yes or No

23. Have you ever somehow known something about a person that you later confirmed was true?

    Yes or No

24. Did you ever dream something that later came to be true?

    Yes or No

25. Have you ever heard, felt, or seen an image of an answer pop into your awareness as you listened to a person talk? (For example, the person might be saying what a bargain they got on an item, and the exact price pops into your mind, and then they confirm it.)

    Yes or No

26. Have you ever noticed you could sense subtle energy, like the next elevator door that was going to open in a large bank of elevators in a high-rise building? Or that there might be an animal on the road during your nighttime drive so you should slow down and use extra caution driving?

    Yes or No

27. Have you ever sensed something about a person as you mingle at a party or work gathering … only to later find out that your initial gut feeling was accurate?

    Yes or No

28. Have you ever felt or sensed someone after they crossed over? Have you felt like their presence was in the room, or that you could sense them in some other way (like receiving a message from them)?

    Yes or No

29. Have you ever had a dream, even if brief, of a loved one who crossed over, that included some of these elements: vivid colors or a light emanating from their face; seeing their vibrant, beaming smile; seeing them as younger, with their best body, and appearance; the person was communicating with you and you knew what they were saying although their mouth wasn't moving; and when you woke up, you felt like you had really interacted with this person?

    Yes or No

30. Do you feel you are more sensitive to substances (medications, caffeine, etc.) than other people?

    Yes or No

* Questions above marked with an asterisk were created using findings from an extensive study of intuitives reported by Belleruth Naparstek (*Your Sixth Sense,* 1997, Harper-Collins, New York, New York); Other helpful resources are audio *Unlocking Intuition*, and www.healthjourneys.com.

Scoring: Give yourself 1 point for each *Yes* answer and 0 points for each *No*.

Total Score _______________

Key:

15 to 30 points – You have had experiences, or possess several typical traits, of people who are found to be intuitive (and possibly even mediumistic, if you had a yes on questions 28 and/or 29).

1 to 14 points – You have had some experiences, or possess some typical traits, of one who is considered somewhat intuitive. This quiz simply measures where you are right now as you take it; so please note that intuition can be developed by anyone through various means over time (noted above).

0 points – While intuition can be developed in anyone, you may be among the population of people stronger in your left brain functions (rational, logical thinking). This quiz measures only where you are today. If you are interested in developing your helpful intuition, find a local class or workshop, or read books on developing intuition.

Please note: This questionnaire/quiz is for entertainment purposes only and is not a definitive indicator of your ability, or a predictor of your accuracy or success, in the fields of intuition, psychic skills, or mediumship. Intuition can be developed in most people, and tends to develop faster in those with natural aptitude who apply dedicated work, practice, and study. Some mediums have written that many who work in the field of psychic mediumship devote a lifetime to developing their abilities. Please note: While some people are intuitive and hear information from their own intuition or spirit guides, others are actually experiencing what some classify as schizophrenia (in this case, seeking professional help from a qualified psychiatric or mental health professional, or getting a referral to one from a medical provider, is advised). Neither this book nor this quiz are suggesting pursuing intuitive development as a path when appropriate mental health professional help is indicated or needed.

Acknowledgments

I want to send an enormous, heartfelt thank you to:

All of you who have helped me along my journey. I know there are many of you, and I am so grateful for all you have contributed to my life. These pages are just a partial list of people I want to thank, so know you *are all so appreciated*!

The woman I call Cheri in this book. There would be no book, or me, if it were not for your kindness and compassion. Perhaps through this book we will reconnect … I would love that! I also thank those skilled medical professionals who helped me come back to a fuller life.

My family for being there before and after this experience in so many ways. My sincere gratitude goes out to all of you for supporting me on the journey of writing this book, and all the calls and visits over the years of support, laughter, and joy. I love you all and am ever more grateful for you in my life—each day—as I realize how precious our connection is.

My spirit loved ones who have given me so many lovely and heartfelt messages over the years since attending my first development circle! My mother and I have created many "frequent flier" miles between our world and the other side as I hear her both heartfelt and other times quite practical ("You need a new bed! Your back is hurting!") messages, as well as the several messages to finish this very book! Thank you for the group message I received via a published medium at a group event (who listed the names, exactly, of many of you in spirit) that encouraged me to "Finish the book about the other side!" That was just priceless to hear your six names in a long string even including your family connections where first three sibling cousins were named (and one spouse), then our in-laws both father and son followed together. Your belief and encouragement that this book be finished helped me move forward.

My friends, current and past. Thank you for being in my life and supporting me on my unusual journey, as well as your ongoing keeping in touch and love. A new source of support that has lit up again like a neon sign is my wonderful high school and college friends who have re-emerged in my life. What a gift to be back in touch with people who have known you for almost your entire life! I'm so grateful for your friendship and support of my mediumship work.

My amazing clients who astound me daily as I am honored and humbled to learn what they are going through as it comes to life from information I hear from both their spirit guides and spirit loved ones.

My Development Circle colleagues both present and past. I cannot say enough about the gifts I received in your presence, and the resulting friendships I cherish, so thank you from the bottom of my heart!

My many helpful teachers, and the ones who have become dear friends. From the early days with Bob and Sheila, to Drew, then Felix Lee Lerma's development circle, then on to a workshop with James Van Praagh, and several classes and workshops with the amazingly talented, excellent teacher Lisa Williams … I cannot thank you all enough! Thank you for encouraging me along those stepping stones of my journey.

My wonderful students. I want to thank you for being so courageous—listening to and developing your intuitive, psychic, and mediumship skills with me in Marin County, California (and in online classes). It's a blast to work with you, hear your questions, and try to help you along your path.

My talented editors, who all had unique roles in reviewing this manuscript. Thank you, Katie Malachuk, for your incredible talent, endless encouragement and enthusiasm, excellent visioning, and editing skills! Thank you, Kelly Notaras, for your editing acumen (and for connecting Katie and me). Thank you, Linda Jay for arriving in the right place at the right time to edit my manuscript (the supermarket … which was the only place I was going beyond working on my book so meeting you in the check-out line was a perfect synchronicity). To Jaene Leonard, who arrived just at the right time as a synchronistic helper as well. I am so grateful to you all, as I just wanted to tell my story.

My skilled team helping me put this book together from cover designer Jon Ianziti (at Ianziti Design) to formatter Val Sherer to photographer Virna Low … thank you all.

Mary, for your incredible support over these years from when I was working frantically downtown to then receiving my apprentice-like training with world-renowned mediums, and now being so encouraging as I work day to day with clients. I cannot thank you enough as you gently encouraged me to finish this book. I always felt like I would write a book so your belief in this project helped me immeasurably.

About the Author

Kay **Fahlstrom** miraculously survived a near-death experience after she was beyond medically established levels of what the human body can endure. While there is no logical reason she should have made it through that harrowing night and lived to tell about it, after her NDE, Kay noticed unexpected gifts and abilities such as premonitions that turned out to prove accurate, psychic knowings, then later mediumship ability, where she could perceive and hear people who had crossed over to the other side of the veil.

Kay enjoys being of service as a medium—bridging the communication with her clients and their departed loved ones. She assists clients in the San Francisco/San Jose Bay Areas and clients worldwide via phone readings. You can hear Kay on many radio programs speaking about her NDE and also giving messages to callers (on both live radio, and Internet radio, with downloadable recordings available).

Kay earned the designation of Certified Spiritual Advisor from the Lisa Williams International School of Spiritual Development, and was also featured on the World Visionary Summit interviews with 26 of the Most Respected Mediums in November 2012.

Kay connects with people and puts them at ease during readings as a professional with integrity, clarity, and passion.

She specializes in giving you messages from not only your loved ones and friends in spirit, but also from your personal spirit guide. After readings, Kay often receives spontaneous feedback that clients now feel a renewed sense of connection, comfort, peace, and healing (and sometimes also a reminder of their spirit person's sense of humor via an inside joke or story)! For more, visit: **www.kayfahlstrom.com**

Contact Kay for a personal reading (by phone for either 30 or 60 minutes; or in person for 60 minutes in Marin County, California—just north of San Francisco) on:

www.kayfahlstrom.com

Use the "Book a Session" page to request a 30- or 60-minute reading, with preferred days of the week and times. Teaching, Life (or Spiritual Journey) Coaching sessions are also available. Like my facebook.com "Kay Fahlstrom Medium" page, and follow Kay Fahlstrom on twitter to learn more.

Or, sign up there for Kay's free newsletters by leaving both your mailing address and email address, as each newsletter covers different information and interesting stories.

Made in the USA
San Bernardino, CA
04 June 2014